People in Language, Vision and the Mind (ONION 2020)

Marseille, France
11 – 16 May 2020

Editors:

Patrizia Paggio
Albert Gatt
Roman Klinger

ISBN: 978-1-7138-1271-5

Printed from e-media with permission by:

Curran Associates, Inc.
57 Morehouse Lane
Red Hook, NY 12571

Some format issues inherent in the e-media version may also appear in this print version.

Association for Computational Linguistics
209 N. Eighth Street
Stroudsburg, Pennsylvania 18360

Phone: 1-570-476-8006
Fax: 1-570-476-0860

acl@aclweb.org

Additional copies of this publication are available from:

Curran Associates, Inc.
57 Morehouse Lane
Red Hook, NY 12571 USA
Phone: 845-758-0400
Fax: 845-758-2633
Email: curran@proceedings.com
Web: www.proceedings.com

LREC 2020 Workshop
Language Resources and Evaluation Conference
11–16 May 2020

People in language, vision and the mind (ONION 2020)

PROCEEDINGS

Editors: Patrizia Paggio, Albert Gatt and Roman Klinger

Proceedings of the LREC 2020 Workshop on People in language, vision and the mind (ONION 2020)

Edited by: Patrizia Paggio, Albert Gatt and Roman Klinger

For more information:
European Language Resources Association (ELRA)
9 rue des Cordelières
75013, Paris
France
http://www.elra.info
Email: lrec@elda.org

Introduction

1 Motivation and Aims of the Workshop

The ability to adequately model and describe people in terms of their body and face is interesting for a variety of language technology applications, e.g., conversational agents and interactive narrative generation, as well as forensic applications in which people need to be identified or their images generated from textual or spoken descriptions. Such systems need resources and models where images associated with human bodies and faces are coupled with linguistic descriptions. Thus, the research needed to develop such datasets and models is placed at the interface between vision and language research, a cross-disciplinary area which has received considerable attention in recent years, e.g., through the activities of the European Network on Integrating Vision and Language (iV&L Net), the 2015–2018 Language and Vision Workshops, the 2018–2019 Workshops on Shortcomings in Vision and Language and the ongoing Multi-Task, Multilingual, Multimodal (Multi3Generation) Generation COST Action.

The aim of this first edition of the ONION workshop was to provide a forum to present and discuss current research focusing on multimodal resources as well as computational and cognitive models aiming to describe people in terms of their bodies and faces, including their affective state as it is reflected physically. Such models might either generate textual descriptions of people, generate images corresponding to descriptions of people, or in general exploit multimodal representations for different purposes and applications. Knowledge of the way human bodies and faces are perceived, understood and described by humans is key to the creation of such resources and models, therefore the workshop also invited contributions where the human body and face are studied from a cognitive, neurocognitive or multimodal communication perspective.

Recent research on the analysis of images and text or the generation of image descriptions focused on datasets which might contain people as a subset; however, we argue that such general multimodal resources are not adequate for the specific challenges posed by applications based on the modelling of human bodies and faces. Descriptions of people are frequent in human communication, for example when one seeks to identify an individual or distinguish one person from another, or in the course of conveying a person's affective state on the basis of facial expression, posture etc. These descriptions are also pervasive in descriptive or narrative text. Depending on the context, they may focus on physical attributes, or incorporate inferred characteristics and emotional elements.

Human body postures and faces are being studied by researchers from different research communities, including those working with vision and language modeling, natural language generation, cognitive science, cognitive psychology, multimodal communication and embodied conversational agents. The workshop aimed to reach out to all these communities to explore the many different aspects of research on the human body and face, including the resources that such research needs, and to foster cross-disciplinary synergy.

2 Contributions

Five papers were accepted for the workshop and are included in this publication. Although this is a small collection, it reflects well the cross-disciplinary nature of the research area which the workshop is targeting.

The paper by Lembke, Folgerø, Andresen and Johansson presents the results of an experimental study which investigates the effect of prototypicality and self-recognition in participants' perception of the attractiveness of facial images. The stimuli used are depictions of Christ that were adapted into more human, gender-specific images and then morphed with individual photos. The results of the study have general implications for the psychological perception of faces that go beyond the study of Christian iconography.

Moving from the study of facial images to analyses of gestural behaviours, the study by Mori, Jokinen and Den deals with the different ways in which hand gestures, head movements and body posture are used in human-robot interaction as opposed to human-human interaction, and also identifies interesting differences between English and Japanese users in the way they use gestural behaviour when interacting with robots.

The paper by Paggio, Agirrezabal, Jongejan and Navarretta reports state-of-the-art results from machine learning classification experiments aimed at the automatic detection of different types of head movement from video-recorded face-to-face dialogues involving twelve different speakers. A number of models are trained using a combination of visual, acoustic and word features in a leave-one-out cross-validation scenario where classifiers are repeatedly trained on data from eleven speakers and tested on the remaining one.

The contribution by Anastasiou, Afkari and Maquil reports the results of a user study on collaborative problem-solving using an interactive tabletop. The focus of the authors is on the role of pointing gestures in low awareness situations, i.e., situations in which a user involved in a task might employ exaggerated manual actions to draw attention and thus raise awareness. The paper argues that the way in which a problem-solving scenario is designed has an effect on the type and frequency of occurring gestures.

Finally, the paper by Schlör, Zehe, Kobs, Veseli, Westermeier, Brübach, Roth, Latoschik and Hotho presents a novel approach to the automatic classification of sentiment in text relying on physiological signals to improve the performance of lexicon-based sentiment classifiers. The physiological signals considered are the heart rate and brain activity of readers recorded while they read short texts that have been annotated with sentiment labels. In addition to reporting the results of the sentiment analysis experiments, the authors make available a dataset that includes sentiment annotations, as well as two types of biofeedback data, namely heart rate and EEG data.

As can be seen from this summary, the papers include a variety of topics, from image perception to the use of gestural behaviour in different scenarios; they employ a range of methods, from experimental analysis to machine learning; they investigate the potential of different kinds of signal from visual and acoustic features to biofeedback data. In conclusion, they touch upon many different aspects of an area of research which we hope future editions of the ONION workshop will contribute to showcase and develop even further.

3 Online presentations

Unfortunately the workshop, which was originally planned to take place on 16 May 2020 in conjunction with the LREC 2020 conference, could not be held as a face-to-face meeting due to the ongoing coronavirus pandemic. Therefore, authors were asked to produce online presentations of the papers. All the presentations will be available from the workshop website at `https://onion2020.github.io/`.

Organizers:

Patrizia Paggio, University of Copenhagen, Denmark and University of Malta, Malta
Albert Gatt, University of Malta, Malta
Roman Klinger, University of Stuttgart, Germany

Program Committee:

Adrian Muscat, University of Malta
Andreas Hotho, University of Würzburg
Andrew Hendrickson, University of Tilburg
Catherine Pelachaud, Institute for Intelligent Systems and Robotics, UPMC and CNRS
Costanza Navarretta, CST, University of Copenhagen
David Hogg, University of Leeds
Diego Frassinelli, University of Konstanz
Isabella Poggi, Roma Tre University
Jordi Gonzalez, Universitat Autònoma de Barcelona
Kristiina Jokinen, National Institute of Advanced Industrial Science and Technology (AIST)
Mihael Arcan, National University of Ireland, Galway
Raffaella Bernardi, CiMEC Trento
Sebastian Padó, University of Stuttgart

Table of Contents

Workshop Program

Prototypes and Recognition of Self in Depictions of Christ
Carla Sophie Lembke, Per Olav Folgerø, Alf Edgar Andresen and Christer Johansson

Analysis of Body Behaviours in Human-Human and Human-Robot Interactions
Taiga Mori, Kristiina Jokinen and Yasuharu Den

Automatic Detection and Classification of Head Movements in Face-to-Face Conversations
Patrizia Paggio, Manex Agirrezabal, Bart Jongejan and Costanza Navarretta

"You move THIS!": Annotation of Pointing Gestures on Tabletop Interfaces in Low Awareness Situations
Dimitra Anastasiou, Hoorieh Afkari and Valérie Maquil

Improving Sentiment Analysis with Biofeedback Data
Daniel Schlör, Albin Zehe, Konstantin Kobs, Blerta Veseli, Franziska Westermeier, Larissa Brübach, Daniel Roth, Marc Erich Latoschik and Andreas Hotho

Proceedings of ONION 2020: Workshop on peOple in laNguage, vIsiOn and the miNd, pages 1–6
Language Resources and Evaluation Conference (LREC 2020), Marseille, 11–16 May 2020

Prototypes and Recognition of Self in Depictions of Christ

Carla-Sophie Lembke[1], Per Olav Folgerø[2], Alf Edgar Andresen[2] & Christer Johansson[2]
[1]Institute of Cognitive Science, University of Osnabrück, Germany
[2]Department of Linguistic, Literary and Aesthetic Studies University of Bergen, Norway

Carla.Lembke@gmx.de, Per.Folgero@uib.no, alf@spotstudio.no, Christer.Johansson@uib.no

Abstract

We present a study on prototype effects. We designed an experiment investigating the effect of adapting a prototypical image towards more human, male or female, prototypes, and additionally investigating the effect of self-recognition in a manipulated image. Results show that decisions are affected by prototypicality, but we find less evidence that self-recognition further enhances perceptions of attractiveness. This study has implications for the psychological perception of faces, and may contribute to the study of Christian imagery.

Keywords: Prototype effects, Self Similarity, Attractiveness, Subjectivity in Face Perception, Experimental Esthetics

1. Introduction

The image of Christ, which is central to both modern and historical Christianity, has undergone many changes to evolve from the historically accurate, middle-eastern carpenter into the modern Hippie Christ that we still see today.

We will try to see this artistic revolution as a mechanism of prototype formation, where repeated exposure to a particular visual category influences our liking or disliking of what we see. Our theory is that the diversity of Christ images may reflect the diversity of the believers by means of artistic adaptation, i.e. painters produced more of the images that appealed most to believers on trustworthiness, attractiveness and identification with self.

Recently, Jackson et al. (2018) have shown that American subjects saw God as being similar to themselves regarding attractiveness and age. We argue that this egocentric bias also plays an important role when it comes to the Christ figure. Therefore, we expect that participants will prefer the images of Christ in which they may recognize features of themselves.

In accordance with this, other studies have documented that mere exposure to a category of stimuli increases the familiarity and liking of that particular domain of stimuli (Reber et al., 2004; Chenier & Winkielman, 2009). Mere exposure has been shown to reduce the identification and classification latencies for stimuli, meaning that it increases the processing speed or fluency.

Another effect of repeatedly seeing similar variants on a theme is that certain forms become prototypical. An everyday example is our tendency to like new retro models of cars, e.g., the Volkswagen Beetle. Winkielman et al. (2006), claim that prototypicality is one of many fluency-enhancing variables. Moreover, they suggest that part of the preference for prototypicality stems from a general mechanism that links fluency and positive values.

When encountering novel faces, we are quick to attribute different traits to them. These attributions happen as quickly as 33 milliseconds after exposure to the face stimulus (Todorov et al., 2009) and the mechanisms responsible for them are already present and reliable in children of 3 to 4 years of age (Cogsdill et al, 2014). To form these impressions, we rely mostly on facial cues, even when other, more relevant, information is available to us (Rezlescu et al., 2012; Oliviola et al., 2014).

There has also been evidence for a bias towards our own facial features when we attribute traits to strangers. The popular observation that couples tend to look alike supports the theory that, with increasing exposure to our face and genetically similar faces over time, we develop an attraction to faces similar to our own (Hinsz, 1989).

Facial similarity also has a positive effect on perceived trustworthiness, group cooperation, and voter preferences in political elections (DeBruine, 2002; DeBruine, 2005; Krupp et al., 2007; Bailenson et al., 2008). In our experiment, we test whether adding the subjects' features to the image of Christ, will make that image more likable as well.

This study explores the idea that the image of Christ has evolved to be more likable by adapting a similarity to the community of believers, including the female believers, by ameliorating hurdles to identify with the image. We hypothesized that this adaption leads to an increase in the attractiveness of the Christ figure. Furthermore, we hypothesized that participants would judge images containing their own image more favorably, even without being conscious of the presence of their own image. This would provide additional empirical evidence for the mere exposure hypothesis, according to which, a participant would prefer an image containing features that are familiar to them.

Previous research on the image of Christ has shown that the Renaissance preference for depicting Christ (as God) en face, is associated with enhancing positive attributions such as being harmonious, caring, trustworthy, inclusive and respected (cf. Folgerø et al 2016a). Furthermore, it has been shown that people may judge the gender of a face from facial proportions between the tip of the nose and the eyebrows (cf. Geniole et al., 2014). For images of Christ, Folgerø et al (2016b) showed in a priming experiment that a brief presentation of a word (*female* or *male*) made participants significantly over-represent a choice of female for images of Christ when primed by the word for female. Images of young men and women were less affected when primed by the opposite gender (ibid). This suggests that not only had the Renaissance image of Christ adapted towards a more Italian / European portrait, but also the painters may have included some female features, adding a more universal androgynous appeal.

2. Method

2.1 Participants

17 students (8 male, 9 female) were initially recruited for the study. Due to the nature of the morphing procedure we used, one female participant was excluded from the study, so there were a total of 16 students, 8 male, and 8 female. All participants gave their informed consent to participate in the study and to have their picture taken and used for publication.

Only 12 participants (aged 18 to 65; mean 26.4 CI[18.2; 34.6]) participated in the final experiment. Thus only 12 images matched the 12 participants for self: 6 male and 6 female.

2.2 Stimuli

We used *Sqirls Morph*, which uses Beier & Neely's (1992) algorithm to morph pictures.

We first chose three renaissance depictions, and one Eastern depiction from the 6th century A.D. of the Holy Face and we produced a *"Christ prototype"* by morphing them (Figure 1).

Furthermore, we created a female and male prototype by combining the pictures of eight female participants and eight male participants, respectively. The male and female prototypes were also combined to produce a human prototype (Figure 2).

We then morphed each picture (the individual pictures and the prototypes) with our Christ prototype to create the stimuli used in the experiment. The 16 individualized Christ images consisted of 80% Christ and 20% the image of the participant (Figure 3).

Figure 1: Creation of the Christ prototype. First four canonical images of Christ are morphed pairwise, and then the pairs are morphed.

Figure 2: Prototypes created from participants. All created by pairwise morphing. Upper row: Female, Human and Male prototypes. The lower row shows the effect of adding the Christ prototype.

Figure 3: Individual participants morphed with the Christ prototype. The alternating rows show first male, then female participants. The morphed pictures consist of 80% Christ prototype and 20% individual picture.

3. Design and Procedure

The experiment has two phases. In the first phase, all participants had their picture taken by a professional photographer in a standardized setting. They sat at an equal distance to the photographer in front of a uniform gray wall directly facing the photographer. The second phase took place six weeks after all pictures had been taken. We created a balanced Round Robin tournament in SuperLab, where an individualized picture (20% from an individual and 80% from the Christ prototype) was presented next to one of the prototypes. All pairs were presented in a different random sequence for each subject. The side of the screen on which the prototype was presented was also randomized (left or right). All combinations were presented exhaustively.

Participants were asked to select the image they found most attractive of the two, as in a *"Hot or Not"* task. All participants were asked to make their responses quickly while remaining accurate. Reaction times were collected, and difficult choices were expected to show increased reaction times.

The experiment is prepared for a follow-up using a *"Visual World"* paradigm, where eye-tracking is used to detect which of the images receive the longest focused attention. Eye-tracking was not available in our lab at the time of our experiment.

4. Results

Four participants did not take part in the final task. That left us with data from 12 participants (aged 18 to 65; mean 26.4 CI[18.2; 34.6]), and gender balanced. Responses that were faster than 300ms were excluded because it would be impossible to process both images and take a decision within that time.

Visualization is performed by **assoc** from the R **vcd** package (cf. Meyer et al. 2003). Prototypes competed against 12 individualized images and the original four images of Christ (cf. Figure 1), each presented one time on the left and one time on the right side.

The female and Christ prototypes won significantly more competitions than any of the other images (Figure 4). The female prototype also shows the fastest reaction times.

Subjects did not show evidence of self-recognition in preference (Figure 5) or decision times. The differences are as in Figure 4. Self tends to win more over the human and male prototypes. In the debriefing after the study, only one participant claimed to have recognized themselves in the images.

Reaction time data was analyzed using a mixed effects model (Kuznetsova et al. 2017) using two fixed factors: the prototype and the choice (for prototype or person). Participants and test items (marked for first or second trial) were used as random factors (explanations for random variance). Furthermore, we used different intercepts for prototypes by each participant and for choice by each item. The reaction times were transformed using a natural logarithm transformation that improves skewed data (long decision times are thought to signal close decisions, but the analysis demands normal distribution). One similar well-known transform is acoustic energy into the decibel scale, which mirrors our perception of sound volume. We investigated some models that included interaction between choice and prototype, but this interaction was not significant and was thus excluded for better model-convergence. The Mixed Effects analysis of the reaction times for decisions (Figure 6) shows a significant effect for choice. When the decision is for a prototype the decision is faster ($F(1,35.6) = 5.3$; $p = 0.027$). There were also differences between prototypes ($F(6,15.2) = 3.9$; $p = 0.015$), most notable PW is faster. We could not confirm any interaction between participant gender and choice (i.e., male subjects seemingly had a larger, but not significant, prototype effect).

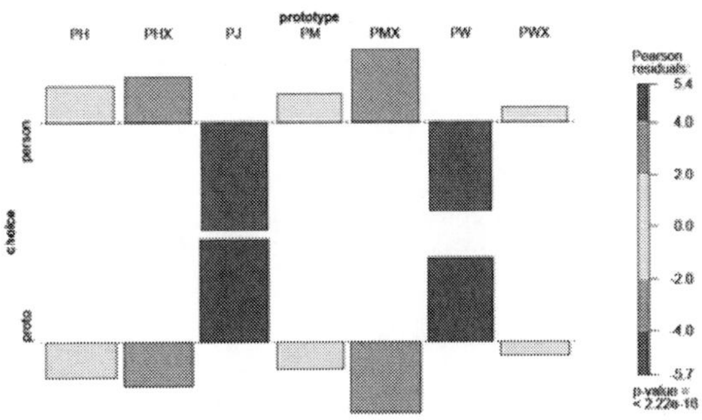

Figure 4: Prototypes are: PH (Human), PHX (Human with Christ), PJ (Jesus Christ), PM (Man), PMX (Man with Christ), PW (Woman), PWX (Woman with Christ). Differences are significant. Red marks cells with lower than expected frequencies, blue are higher than expected. $\chi^2_{(6)}=154.4$, $p<0.001$, $\Phi_c=0.096$

	PH	PHX	PJ	PM	PMX	PW	PWX
PE	241	254	138	236	271	151	227
PR	220	214	335	227	190	319	237

Table 1: Frequency of choice for person (PE) or prototype (PR), competition for each prototype.

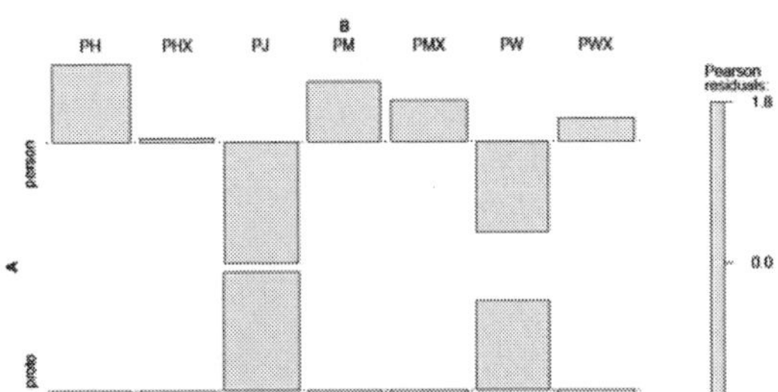

Figure 5: Same graph restricted to choices between *self* (=person) and *prototype*. $\chi^2_{(6)}=16.5$, $p=0.011$, $\Phi_c=0.140$.

	PH	PHX	PJ	PM	PMX	PW	PWX
PE	16	12	5	15	14	7	13
PR	8	12	18	9	10	17	11

Table 2: Table 1 restricted for choices between *self* (PE) and a *prototype* (PR)

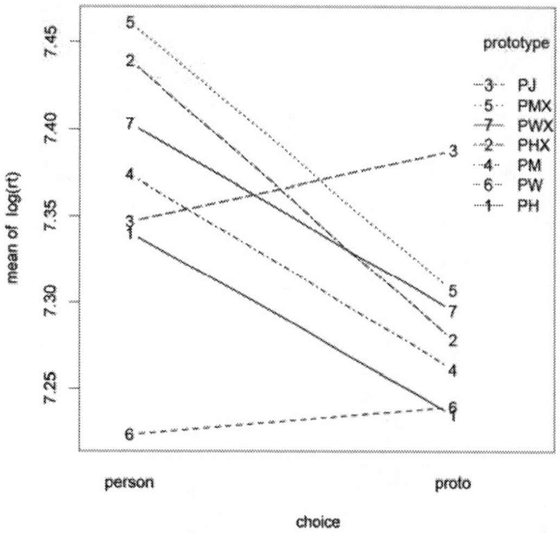

Figure 6: Response times (natural logarithms). Prototypes are generally faster when the decision is *for* the prototype, with exceptions for the Jesus Christ prototype (PJ) and the woman prototype (PW).

A model test of the residuals shows an excellent fit to a normal distribution up to +2 quantiles, but the larger residuals give room for improvement (Figure 7).

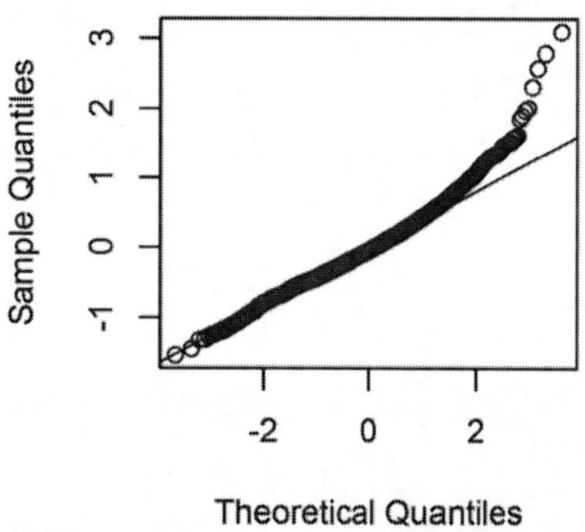

Figure 7: Model test of residuals shows a good fit.

Contrary to our hypothesis, we did not find any significant tendency for participants to rate their own disguised image as more attractive. Instead, there was an insignificant tendency in the opposite direction. One interpretation is that we simply did not have enough statistical power since four of our initial 16 participants were not able to participate in the final task. Alternatively, our subjects might have judged their own image as slightly less attractive than the ratings from others.

5. Ethical Considerations & Discussion

Our work poses many ethical questions that we would like to briefly examine.

In general, as we are working with personal images, special care must be taken that the subjects stay anonymous. It is every researcher's responsibility to inform all participants of what exactly will happen with their images after the study itself has come to an end.

Explicit consent was gathered from all participants, also regarding the use of images. Special care should nevertheless be taken when publishing the data. In our case, we decided to only publish the images of the morphed face stimuli in order to keep the subjects' anonymity intact. The debriefing of our subjects verified the validity of this method as only one of our subjects reported that they had recognized themselves in any of the presented pictures.

Since we are using images of Christ, we realized that this might be sensitive in a religious setting. However, the image of Christ is widespread and familiar to all of our subjects. We discussed this in the debriefing with our participants, with no negative reactions. Participants were generally positive about the underlying theme of finding something holy in everyone.

This study is thus limited, and therefore generalization of our findings may be less than absolute. Our small subject pool may not be representative outside of our local student population. Minorities are difficult to represent fairly within a study limited to a dozen subjects. An option to increase subject diversity is to partner with other researchers, taking particular caution to safely sharing the images in order to protect the subjects' interests.

As with any other field of science, there are distinct ethical concerns that arise when we research human attributes. It is essential for all researchers to identify these ethical issues to the best of their abilities.

In a small study, it is essential to limit the number of variables in order to have better control of variance. Many factors affect attractiveness. Our study was open to everyone, and thus we could not balance all possible features. Skin tone is one feature that has been linked to attractiveness, and a lighter skin tone is often reported as more attractive (Vera Cruz 2018). In our study, the participants were all similar in skin tone, which was toned down further by the morphing process. Similarly, blue eyes became a tone of brown after morphing. It is conceivable that both skin tone and eye color may affect ratings of attractiveness. In our experience, when we observed art interpretations of Christ from the relevant period it is obvious that Christ has a lighter skin tone and bluer eyes in Northern Europe than in Southern Europe, which may be interpreted as an adaptation to the local populations. In a larger study, the relative importance of features can be estimated. Symmetry and androgyny may be more important factors than skin tone and eye color. However, we do find dark-hued representations of both the Mother Virgin and Christ. A dark skin tone in Europe points at an anti-adaptation for the Black Madonna (cf. https://en.wikipedia.org/wiki/Black_Madonna), and an adaptation for the Christos Negros of Central America (cf. https://en.wikipedia.org/wiki/Cristos_Negros_of_Central_America_and_Mexico).

A possible hypothesis is that facial anatomy and symmetry are more important than skin tone in regards to how people identify with a representation.

We also know from the Thatcher-effect that people perceive features of a face separately. Yamaguchi et al (1995) investigated features of the face that affect perception of gender, and found that eyebrows and outline of the face were important features. They found a bias towards own gender in Japanese students, which we have not detected for Norwegian students in our lab. In our own research, we found that Renaissance portraits of Christ had facial proportions (width between eyes vs. length between eyebrows and tip of nose) that were more typical of portraits of female subjects.

It is also interesting to note the deep history of morphing and composite (prototype) effects. Galton (1878) used early photographic techniques to overlay portraits in order to form a composite image. Galton describes a physical procedure for normalizing the pictures by aligning some fix points such as pupils of the eyes. He notes: "... that the features of the composites are much better looking than those of the components." Thus, he is one of the first to notice the prototype-effect on beauty, as the composites get more symmetrical and blemishes are blurred out. Galton also noticed that individual characteristics could be hard to perceive across ethnic classes, as we tend to remember deviances from a familiar composite prototype formed by experience. In a sense, the prototype of the other could be just as distant as the individual, with implications for witness psychology.

6. Conclusions

Both female and Christ prototypes were judged as more attractive (by winning more competitions). Prototypes were processed more fluently, as reflected in their reaction times. The female prototype displayed the fastest decision times, and was more frequently chosen, which may be interpreted as easier to process and possibly more attractive to our participants. Being part of all the individualized images made decisions for the Christ prototype harder, but this prototype was more frequently chosen. The findings support our central hypothesis concerning the adaption of the image of Christ towards a cognitively more pleasing image. An advantage for female features was detected, supporting earlier results on feminine features in the image of Christ (cf. Folgerø et al. 2016b). In Folgerø et al. (2016b), the stimulus was restricted to a section of the face between the tip of the nose and the eyebrows, and yet people showed effects for correct identification of gender, as well as recognition of Christ as a female when primed with "woman."

However, we did not find that images containing features of self were judged as more *attractive*. Following DeBruin (2005), we suggest that the results would have been different if we had asked the participants to judge *trustworthiness* instead of attractiveness. In ongoing data-collection, we note that a majority of our participants now claim, in debriefings, to have recognized themselves in a similar task that includes selecting the face they trust the most. More research is needed to investigate if trustworthiness is more associated with self-similarity.

7. Acknowledgements

The participation of Carla Lembke was made possible by an EU Erasmus+ Traineeship. Alf Edgar Andresen is a former colleague and a professional photographer, who has prepared photographs and morphed images. Without Alf this work could not have been accomplished. The work has been performed at the Humanities Lab at the University of Bergen (https://www.uib.no/en/rg/humlab). Our colleague Tori Larsen provided detailed feedback on the text. We would also like to thank four anonymous reviewers for useful suggestions, which resulted in an extended discussion on the role of skin tone and ethnicity and some clarifications that we think have benefitted our presentation.

Bibliographical References

Bailenson, J., Iyengar, S., Yee, N. & Collins, N. 2008. Facial similarity between voters and candidates causes influence, *Public Opinion Quarterly*, 72(5), 935-961. https://doi.org/10.1093/poq/nfn064

Beier, T. & Neely, S. 1992. Feature-based image metamorphosis, *Computer Graphics,* 26(2), 35–42. https://doi.org/10.1145/133994.134003

Chenier, T. & Winkielman, P. 2009. The origins of aesthetic pleasure: Processing fluency and affect in judgment, body, and the brain. Ch. 14 in Martin Skov & Oshin Vartanian (Eds) *Neuroaesthetics*, Routledge / Baywood, 275-289.

Cogsdill, E., Todorov, A., Spelke, E. & Banaji, M. 2014. Inferring character from faces: A developmental study. *Psychological science*, 25(5). 1132-1139. https://doi.org/10.1177/0956797614523297

DeBruine, L. 2002. Facial resemblance enhances trust. *Proceedings of the Royal Society B: Biological Sciences*, 269(1498), 1307-1312.

DeBruine, L. 2005. Trustworthy but not lust-worthy: Context-specific effects of facial resemblance. *Proceedings of the Royal Society B: Biological Sciences*, 272(1566), 919-922.

Folgerø, P., Hodne, L., Johansson, C., Andresen, A., Sætren, L.C., Specht, K., Skaar, Ø.O. & Reber, R. 2016a. Effects of Facial Symmetry and Gaze Direction on Perception of Social Attributes: A Study in Experimental Art History, *Frontiers in Human Neuroscience*, 10, September 2016. https://doi.org/10.3389/fnhum.2016.00452

Folgerø, P., Johansson, C. & Andresen, A. 2016b. Transgender Priming in Medieval Europe, XXIV. *Conference of the International Association of Empirical Aesthetics*, Vienna, Austria. August 29 – September 1. 2016.

Galton, F. 1878. Composite portraits. *Journal of the Anthropological Institute of Great Britain and Ireland, 8*, 132–142. http://www.galton.org/essays/1870-1879/galton-1879-jaigi-composite-portraits.pdf

Geniole, S.N., Molnar, D.S., Carré, J.M. & McCormick, C.M. 2014. The facial width-to-height ratio shares stronger links with judgments of aggression than with judgments of trustworthiness. *Journal of Experimental Psychology: Human Perception and Performance, 40*(4), 1526–1541. https://doi.org/10.1037/a0036732

Hinsz, V. 1989. Facial resemblance in engaged and married couples, *Journal of Social and Personal Relationships*, 6, 223-229.

Jackson, J., Hester, N. & Gray, K. 2018. The faces of God in America: Revealing religious diversity across people and politics. *PloS one,* 13.6 (2018): e0198745.

Krupp, D., Debruine, L. & Barclay, P. 2008. A cue of kinship promotes cooperation for the public good. *Evolution and Human Behavior*, 29(1), 49-55.

Kuznetsova, A., Brockhoff, P. & Christensen, R. 2017. lmerTest Package: Tests in Linear Mixed Effects Models. Journal of Statistical Software, 82(13), 1–26. https://doi.org/10.18637/jss.v082.i13

Meyer, M., Zeileis, A. & Hornik, K. 2003. Visualizing independence using extended association plots. Proc. of the 3rd International Workshop on Distributed Statistical Computing, K. Hornik, F. Leisch, A. Zeileis (eds.), ISSN 1609-395X. http://www.R-project.org/conferences/DSC-2003/Proceedings/

Olivola, C., Funk, F. & Todorov, A. 2014. Social attributions from faces bias human choices. *Trends in Cognitive Sciences*,18, 566-570.

Reber, R., Schwarz, N. & Winkielman, P. 2004. Processing fluency and aesthetic pleasure: Is beauty in the perceiver's processing experience? *Personality and social psychology review,* 8(4), 364-382.

Rezlescu, C., Duchaine, B., Olivola, C. & Chater, N. 2012. Unfakeable facial configurations affect strategic choices in trust games with or without information about past behavior. *PloS one,* 7, e34293 https://doi.org/10.1371/journal.pone.0034293

Todorov, A., Pakrashi, M. & Oosterhof, N. 2009. Evaluating faces on trustworthiness after minimal time exposure. *Social Cognition,* 27(6), 813-833.

Vera Cruz, G. 2018. The impact of face skin tone on perceived facial attractiveness: A study realized with an innovative methodology, *The Journal of Social Psychology,* 158:5, pp. 580-590. https://doi.or/10.1080/00224545.2017.1419161

Winkielman, P., Halberstadt, J., Fazendeiro, T., & Catty, S. 2006. Prototypes are attractive because they are easy on the mind. *Psychological Science*, 17. 799-806. https://doi.org/10.1111/j.1467-9280.2006.01785.x

Yamaguchi, M. K., Hirukawa, T., & Kanazawa, S. 1995. Judgment of gender through facial parts. *Perception,* 24, 563–575.

Proceedings of ONION 2020: Workshop on peOple in laNguage, vIsiOn and the miNd, pages 7–14
Language Resources and Evaluation Conference (LREC 2020), Marseille, 11–16 May 2020

Analysis of Body Behaviours in Human-Human and Human-Robot Interactions

Taiga Mori*†, Kristiina Jokinen†, Yasuharu Den‡

*Graduate School of Humanities and Studies on Public Affairs, Chiba University
‡Graduate School of Humanities, Chiba University
1-33 Yayoicho, Inage-ku, Chiba 263-8522, Japan

†AI Research Center, AIST Tokyo Waterfront
2-4-7 Aomi, Koto-ku, Tokyo 135-0064, Japan

mori-taiga@aist.go.jp, kristiina.jokinen@aist.go.jp, den@chiba-u.jp

Abstract

We conducted preliminary comparison of human-robot (HR) interaction with human-human (HH) interaction conducted in English and in Japanese. As the result, body gestures increased in HR, while hand and head gestures decreased in HR. Concerning hand gesture, they were composed of more diverse and complex forms, trajectories and functions in HH than in HR. Moreover, English speakers produced 6 times more hand gestures than Japanese speakers in HH. Regarding head gesture, even though there was no difference in the frequency of head gestures between English speakers and Japanese speakers in HH, Japanese speakers produced slightly more nodding during the robot's speaking than English speakers in HR. Furthermore, positions of nod were different depending on the language. Concerning body gesture, participants produced body gestures mostly to regulate appropriate distance with the robot in HR. Additionally, English speakers produced slightly more body gestures than Japanese speakers.

Keywords: human-human and human-robot interactions, hand gestures, head gestures, body gestures, Japanese and English

1. Introduction

In recent years, multimodal interaction has become a much studied research area and many investigations have been conducted to widen our understanding of human behaviour and interaction dynamics. Research concerns multimodal resources and models on various aspects of interaction associated with the use of whole body and the combination of visual and auditive modalities, and recently also novel technology has offered interesting possibilities for analysing human behaviour in an accurate manner: the use of video, motion capture, eye-tracker, and many sensor devices provide data which can be used as input to bigdata and machine-learning calculations in order to establish accurate correlations and relations among the modalities. Moreover, novel applications such as interactive social robots have also become common, and in order to develop more natural systems that can understand human behaviour as well as produce expressive and engaging behaviour, it is important to study multimodal communication in situations with humans and other interactive agents. For instance, co-speech gesturing is important in making one's presentation natural, engaging, and expressive, and it is also important to be able to detect and interpret the relevant signals so as to understand the partner's communicative intentions.

In this paper, we focus on gesturing to study spoken interactions in a practical context of instructing or giving advice to a colleague, about how to perform a particular care-giving task. In our research we have selected hand gestures and head nodding as the primary object of study. There is already much research on how gestures and nods function in human communication, while coordination of speech and gestures is less studied, especially for the purpose of human-robot interaction. Important goals of our research are thus related to deepening our knowledge of the use of co-speech gestures in interaction, and to investigate how to build models for enabling more natural interaction with robots. Such multimodal interaction models can be applied in human-robot interaction. We annotated the gestures using a modified MUMIN annotation scheme (Allwood et al. 2007). The scheme uses gesture features divided into form and function features, and it is described more in Section 3 and Section 8. The research question concerns how to use gesturing in grounding information and creating mutual understanding of the discussion topic, i.e. how the user's gestures can be used to establish an appropriate way to continue the interaction. We will especially study differences between human-human and human-robot interaction and also compare interactions conducted in English and in Japanese. Our hypotheses with respect to gesturing are:

1) There are more body movements in HH than in HR dialogues.
2) In particular, there are more hand gestures in HH than in HR dialogues, and there are more body movements in HR than in HH.
3) There are more body movements in dialogues conducted in English than in Japanese.
4) There are more body movements when speaking than in listening.
5) There is correlation between body movements and the person's perception of the dialogue in general.

We will also combine presentation of spoken information with gesture and (later) eye-gaze information to design the system's behaviour with respect to multimodal information. For instance, in the robot's listening side suitable dialogue strategies are available to predict the user's understanding or misunderstanding based on their gesture reaction and to specify the presented information appropriately. On the generation side, dialogue strategies include multimodal signals to provide a relevant response and present information and mark the speaker's continued attention to the partner. This kind of grounding in interaction (Clark and Schaefer 1987) is important in understanding the partner's intentions and making one's own intentions known, i.e. to enable smooth interaction. It is hypothesized that the robot's perceived cooperation and grounding of information improves naturalness of its spoken interaction. This is crucial especially in long-term interaction (Heylen et al. 2010) and in various applications related to social robotics where the robot is to act like a co-worked or companion and provide information to the user as well support natural, friendly interaction: the robot's detection of the user's understanding and misunderstanding is important to provide expressive interaction which supports emotionally satisfying and pleasant interaction (Kanda et al. 2004; Beck et al 2010). We were interested in the user's and the robot's mutual understanding process, and especially how the non-expected and misunderstood situations are reflected in the user's gesture patterns, to be able to use this information in designing the robot's interaction strategy.

This paper is structured as follows. First, a short overview of relevant gesture studies is reviewed in Section 2, then the data and annotation scheme are presented briefly in Section 3, and preliminary results shown in Section 4. Next, some methodological issues as well as ethical issues related to the monitoring and data collection in the context of interactive systems are discussed in Section 5, and conclusions are drawn in Section 6. Finally, specific annotation scheme is attached to Section 8.

2. Overview of Previous Work

In linguistic interaction, speech is commonly associated with gesturing (Kendon 2004) and co-speech gestures have been studied from the point of view of turn-taking (Duncan 1972; Streek 2009), iconic gestures and description (Lis and Navarretta 2014), pointing gestures (Jokinen 2010), gestures and multimodal information (Paggio and Navarretta 2013), gestures and neurocognitive processes (Kita et al. 2017), and intercultual comparison (Navarretta et al. 2012; Endrass et al. 2011). Also, in integrating more natural interaction possibilities for a robot (Jokinen and Wilcock 2014; Ono et al. 2001). Automatic analysis platforms have also been developed (Heimerl et al. 2019) and machine learning is used to study interpersonal dynamics (Baltrušaitis et al. 2019). In human-robot interaction (HRI), multimodal issues are also important as speaking robots start to appear in homes, public spaces, and work. The robot's communicative patterns are still rather inflexible, and user evaluations usually point to the robot's inflexible feedback strategies and monotonous engagement with the human. Social robots range from speaking heads (Alexa, Google) to more dialogue-oriented interactive systems for task-based scenarios (Sidner et al. 2015; Jokinen et al., 2018) and although much research is conducted on speech-based HRI, low utilization of multimodal signal in HRI still constrains the understanding of the role of social signals in HR.

3. Data and Annotation

The data is from the AICO Corpus (Jokinen, 2020) which is available for cooperative research at AIST. It consists of 30 participants, 20 native Japanese and 10 English speakers with backgrounds in Europe, US and South-East Asia, of which 10 are women. They are students and researchers, aged 20-60, and they have experience on IT but no experience on robots.

Figure 1 shows the experimental setup. Each participant had two sessions one with a human partner and one with a robot partner for about 10 minutes respectively, so altogether there are 60 interactions, i.e. 30 human-human (HH) and 30 human-robot (HR) interactions. In HH session, one of the experimenters played the role of the human partner and the Nao robot played the role of the robot partner in HR session. Other experimenters monitored the session from the next room to intervene when problems arise. Data was collected using video camera, Kinect, eye-tracker and a questionnaire about impression on the robot. The setup is described in more detail in Ijuin et al. (2019) and Jokinen (2019). This data enables us to compare interaction patterns across the human and agent partners. In this paper we compare the human-human and human-robot interactions, and also draw some observations concerning interactions conducted in Japanese and in English.

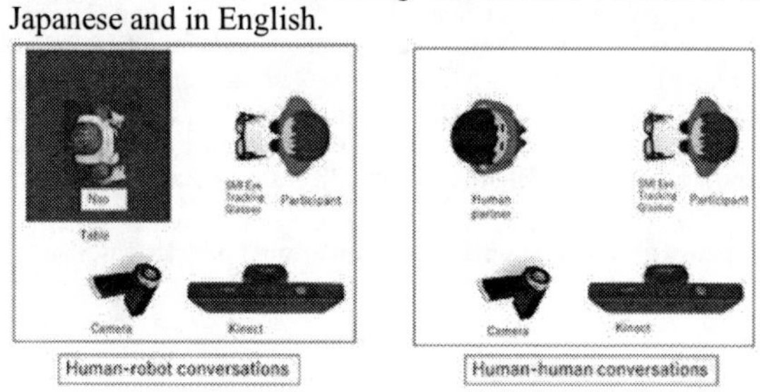

Figure 1: The experimental setup

Gestures can be classified according to a modified version of the MUMIN annotation scheme (Allwood et al. 2007), which is based on the gesture form (e.g., up-open, curled-fingers and extended-finger) and the gesture function (e.g., iconic, deictic and emblem gestures). For the full set of annotation categories, see Section 8. At the moment, 19 interactions have been annotated and 16 of them were used for the following analyses. Table 1 shows the breakdown of the analysed data.

Japanese				English			
HH		HR		HH		HR	
M	F	M	F	M	F	M	F
2	1	4	1	2	2	2	2

Table 1: Breakdown of analysed data

M and F mean male and female participant's number respectively.

4. Gesture and Body Posture Analysis

4.1 Hand Gestures

4.1.1 Mean Frequency of Hand Gestures

Figure 2 shows the mean frequency of hand gestures. As can be seen, hand gestures considerably decreased in HR, which is in accordance with our hypothesis. Considering the language differences, it is interesting that even though the English speakers produced 6 times more hand gestures in HH than the Japanese, their difference is not so big in HR. The similar trends between English and Japanese in HR is because both English and Japanese speakers produced only self-directed gestures in HR, such as touching a table or scratching one's body. This implies that for realizing natural interaction with a robot, it is necessary to focus first on eliciting gestures from the user rather than on recognizing gestures.

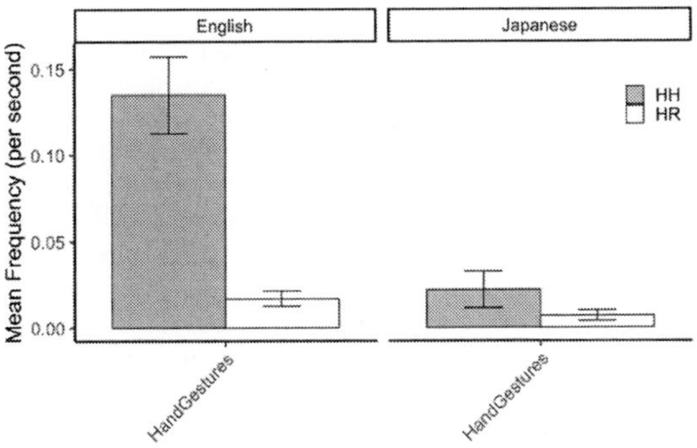

Figure 2: Mean frequency of hand gestures. Error bars show the standard errors.

4.1.2 Form

The most frequent hand gesture form for the English speakers was *curled-fingers* in both HH and HR sessions (Figure 3). However, in HH, other forms also occurred, while this form was almost the only one observed in HR. In our scheme, *curled-fingers* is defined as the default form realized without any effort, in contrast to the *opening a palm* or *pointing* (Table 2). That is, English speakers made more complex hand forms in HH. Similar pattern was also observed for the Japanese speakers, although they produced less hand gestures than English speakers. Considering the language differences, English speakers produced twice more gestures than Japanese in almost all hand form. On the basis of this result, it can be said that English interaction is more dependent on hand gestures than Japanese interaction. This suggests that robots have to recognize more various hand gesture forms in English than in Japanese.

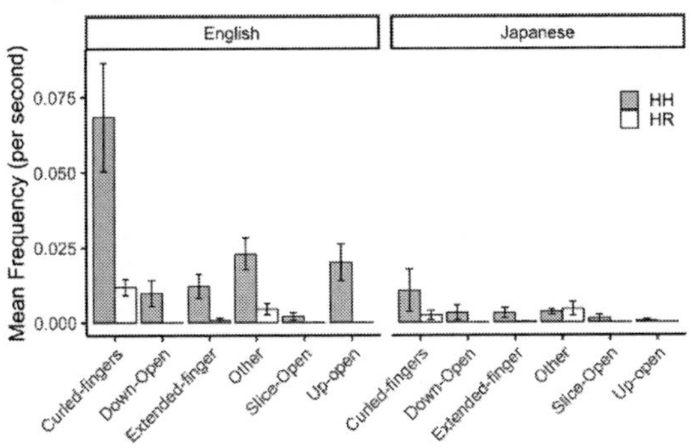

Figure 3: Mean frequency of hand gesture forms

4.1.3 Function

As with the gesture forms, the functions of hand gestures were also more diverse in HH than in HR (Figure 4). Almost all gestures that were produced in HR are classified as *adapter* gestures, such as leaning one's body weight onto a table or touching one's body. As *rhythmic, iconic, deictic* and *emphasis* gestures are obviously more interactive than *adapter* gestures, it can be concluded that the participants mostly produced other-directed gestures in HH. Considering the language differences, English speakers produced more rhythmic gestures than Japanese, suggesting that prosodic information including intonation and rhythm might be more important in English than in Japanese. Another important implication is that Japanese speakers might emphasise important point in other modality because they produced fewer *emphasis* hand gesture. In conclusion, because Japanese speakers produce less other-directed hand gestures than English speakers, the need for robots to accurately recognize hand gesture might be lower in Japanese than in English.

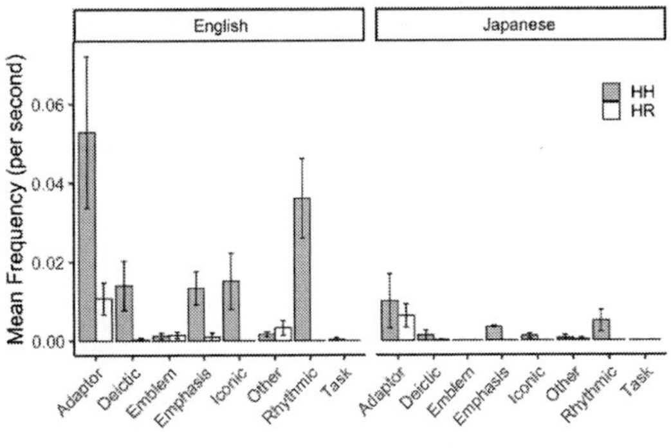

Figure 4: Mean frequency of hand gesture functions

4.1.4 Trajectory

Concerning the trajectory of the gestures, the *straight* trajectory is the most frequent in HH interactions: *complex* trajectories occurred only about half as many as the *straight* ones (Figure 5). However, in HR interactions, *complex* trajectory is not observed at all. This observation is consistent with the fact that there are very few complex gesture forms in HR. *Complex* gesture trajectories and forms could represent more rich information visually, but they would demand more cognitive costs in terms of production, recognition and interpretation. In the case of HR interaction, the participants seem to "save" the cost of producing complex gestures, because they did not regard the robot as a partner who can recognize rich visual information. In order to elicit hand gestures from humans in HR interaction, the robot should produce gestures naturally so that the human partners can assume and perceive that it can interact with them tactfully in visual modality.

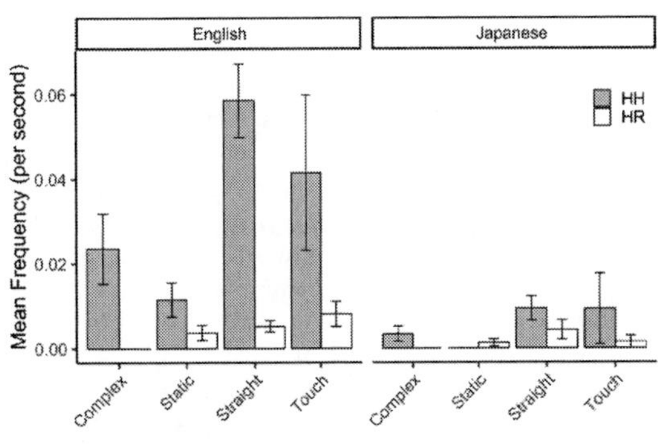

Figure 5: Mean frequency of hand gesture trajectories

4.1.5 Handedness

Based on the results concerning the hand gesture form and trajectory, it can be predicted that there would be less gestures using both hands than gestures using a single hand, because both hand gestures would be more costly. However, contrary to the prediction, the difference between single and both hands gesturing was not so big either in HH nor in HR (Figure 6). This suggests that both hand gestures cannot be omitted into single hand gestures because they are determined by their function and the content of the gesture expression. For instance, one participant represented 'low' and 'high' with the left hand and the right hand respectively; this gesture could not be represented only with a single hand.

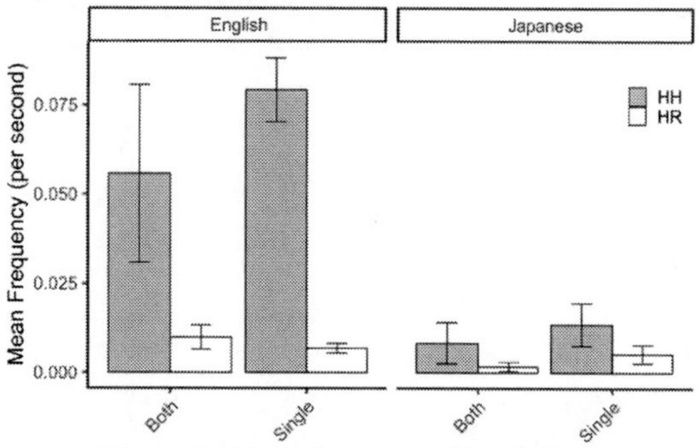

Figure 6: Mean frequency of handedness

4.1.6 Repetition

Similarly to the handedness, there was no difference between *single* and *repeated* gestures in either sessions (Figure 7). *Single* gestures were frequently observed in *emphasis* gestures, while *repeated* gestures were frequently observed in *rhythmic* gestures.

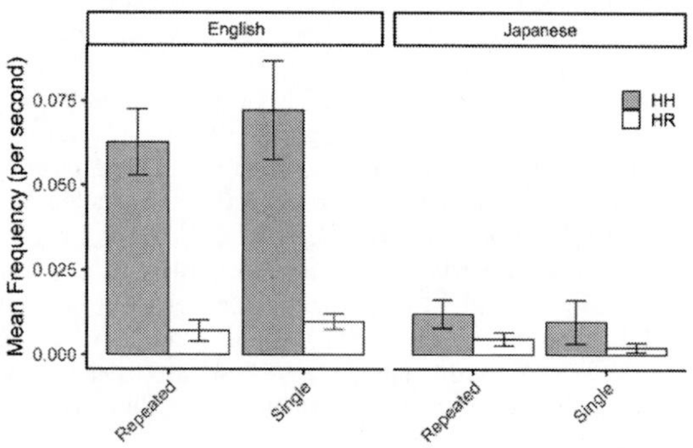

Figure 7: Mean frequency of hand gesture repetition

4.2 Head Gestures

4.2.1 Mean Frequency of Head Gestures

Figure 8 shows mean frequency of head gestures. As can be seen, head gestures decreased in HR in a similar manner as hand gestures. While there was not so big difference between English and Japanese in HH, Japanese speakers produced slightly more head gestures in HR than English speakers.

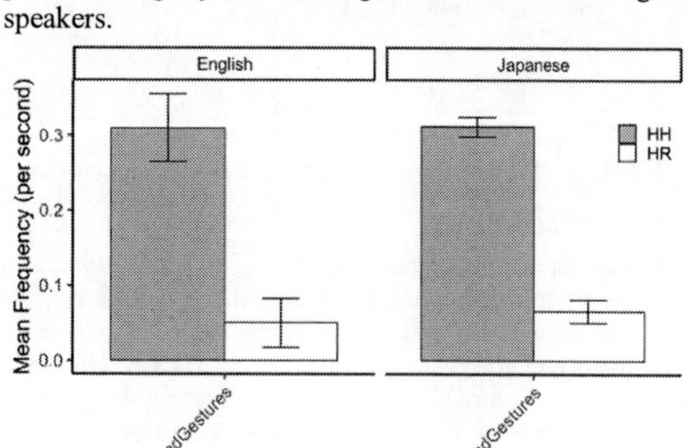

Figure 8: Mean frequency of head gesture

4.2.2 Form

Nod gestures were remarkably most frequent in HH (Figure 9). Although Maynard (1989) showed that native Japanese speakers tend to nod more frequently than American English speakers, there was no big difference between Japanese and English in HH. The following point can be given as reasons for this. Because not all English participants were native speakers, their interactional manner in their first language produced this incoherent result. As evidence for this, individual differences were larger in English speaking interactions than in Japanese interactions. On the other hand, nod gestures observed in HR were slightly more frequent in Japanese. One possible reason is that the Japanese speakers behaved with the robot in the same way as they always do with the human partner. Moreover, Japanese nodded with a response token overlapping partner's utterance while English speakers nodded silently. It is interesting to analyse if the Japanese nodded at the same position in the partner's utterance in HHI and HRI, and also to analyse the relationship between response token and head gestures.

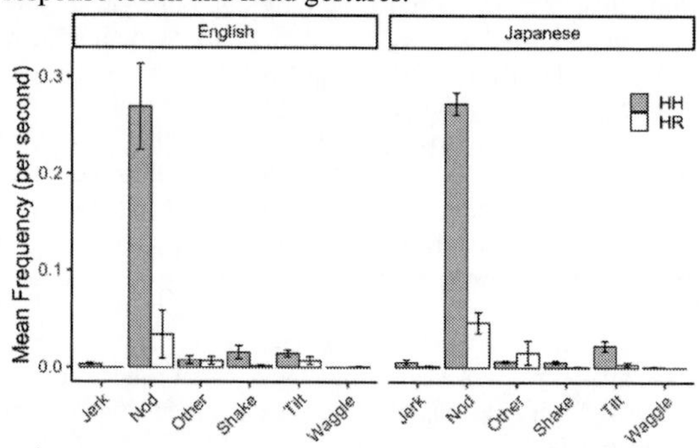

Figure 9: Mean frequency of head gesture forms

4.2.3 Function

Regardless of language, *acknowledge* gestures were most frequent in HH, and *emphasis* gestures were the second most frequent gestures (Figure 10). On the other hand, in HR, the *acknowledge* and *adapter* gestures were relatively more frequent than other functions. Almost all *acknowledge* gestures were observed as *nod*. In HR, Japanese speakers produced more *acknowledge* gestures than English, due to the fact that the Japanese did not nod only during human speaking but also when the robot speaking. Japanese speakers also produced more nods towards the end of their utterance than the English speakers. This implies that Japanese monitored the partner more strictly to elicit gestures when they had the turn. That is to say, robots have to recognize and response to that.

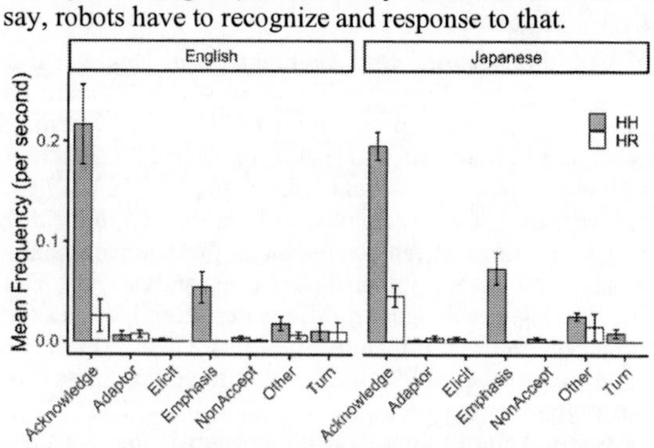

Figure 10: Mean frequency of head gesture functions

4.2.4 Repetition

While *repeated* gestures were more frequent than *single* ones in HH, this tendency was reversed in HR (Figure 11). Although *repeated* gestures would involve more physical cost than *single* ones, they also enable us to represent strong empathy or deep understanding to a speaker. Participants intended to give strong encouraging feedback to the partner in HH, but they saved the cost when talking to the robot. Moreover, the fact that this tendency is common to English and Japanese speakers implies that the function of repetition is common to English and Japanese. In other words, robots can interpret the repetition of head gestures in the same way between Japanese and English.

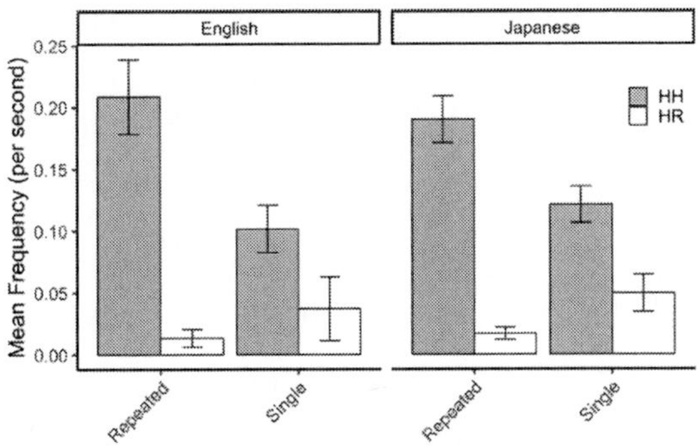

Figure 11: Mean frequency of head gesture repetition

4.3 Body Gestures

4.3.1 Mean Frequency of Body Gestures

Figure 12 shows mean frequency of body gestures. While hand and head gestures were more frequent in HH, body gestures were more frequent in HR. This result suggests that it is more necessary for robots to recognize body gestures than hand and head gestures. Even though there was not so big difference, English speakers produced more body gestures than Japanese in accord with hypothesis.

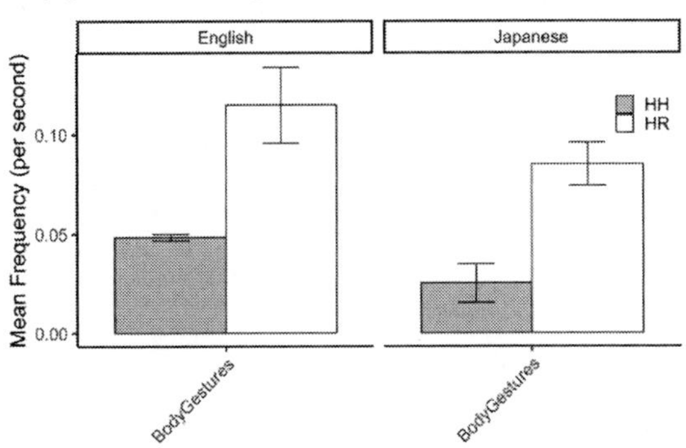

Figure 12: Mean frequency of body gestures

4.3.2 Form

Forward movements were observed most frequently in HR (Figure 13). For instance, participants leaned toward the robot when they spoke to the robot. They sometimes spoke to the robot in the middle of its utterance even though it was programmed to light up and sound on the end and start of its turn. This implies that they could not use unnatural cues for turn-taking. On the other hand, *backward* movements were observed, for instance when participants leaned backward because the robot failed to catch their words or behaved unexpectedly, and then returned to the original position in order to restart the conversation. These behaviours may imply that they made interactive formation with the robot like an F-formation (Kendon 2004), i.e. they broke away from the interactive situation when the robot failed to behave as expected. As for other movements, such as moving sideways and changing body weight from one foot to another were observed in both HH and HR, but shaking one's legs angrily was observed in only HR.

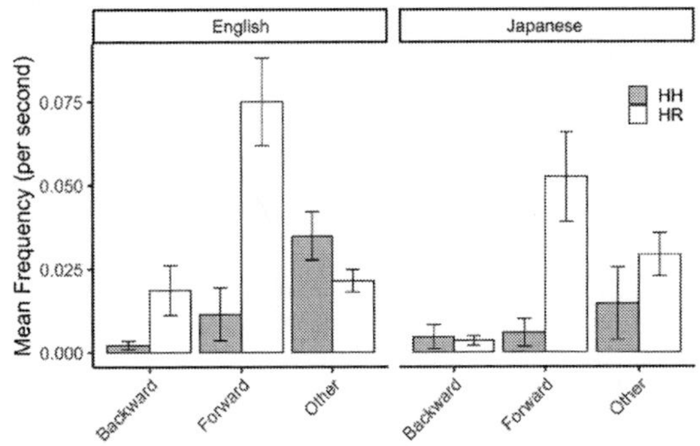

Figure 13: Mean frequency of body gesture forms

4.3.3 Function

The most frequent body function was *better contact* in HR regardless of language (Figure 14). Participants were able to regulate appropriate distance each other in HH, however they had to do that by oneself in HR, and which involves cost for humans. It is desirable for robots in the future to recognize and regulate appropriate distance to humans oneself. Moreover, although frequency of *adapter* gestures was equal in HH and in HR, the gestures occurred in different occasions. While participants frequently changed their body posture when nervous in HH, they shook their legs in frustration to the robot's failure in HR. The data, although small to draw generalisations, shows that male participants looked irritated and produced more *adapter* gestures when the robot failed to catch their words, while females just behaved as confused or laughed. Based on this, it can be assumed that females perceived the robot as more "social entity" than males.

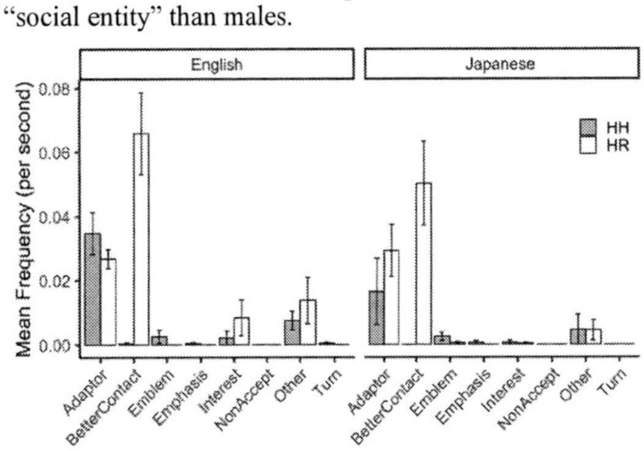

Figure 14: Mean frequency of body gesture functions

4.3.4 Repetition

Single gestures were most frequent in HH and in HR (Figure 15). They were observed when participants leaned forward with each utterance to speak to the robot, or they changed their body weight from one foot to another. *Repeated* gestures were observed as swaying body co-occurred with *rhythmic* hand gesture, or shaking legs from stress. *Static* gestures were observed when participants continued a head forward posture for a few second to reduce physical costs of leaning forward repeatedly. It also suggests that it is larger cost to regulate physical distance. Consequently, body gestures might have involved transmission of information rather than content of interaction, and reflected their mental state such as being nervous or frustrating because they have less expressiveness than hand and head gestures.

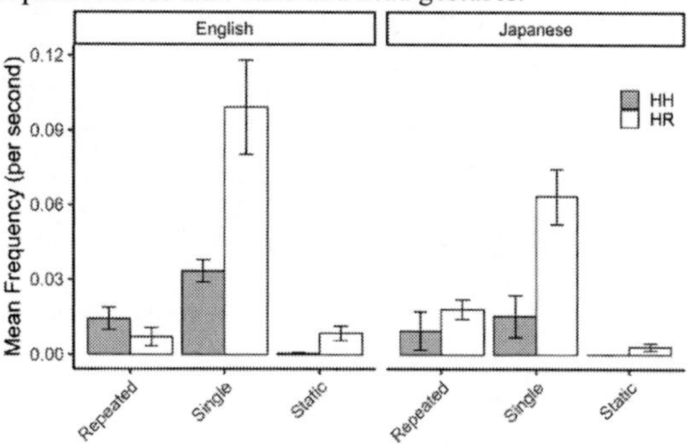

Figure 15: Mean frequency of body gesture repetition

5. Future Work

Since the annotated data is fairly small, we first aim to finish the annotations so to provide a solid basis for the statistical analysis. In the next step of the research, we plan to study time correlation between speech and multimodal gesturing (co-speech hand gesturing, nodding, and body movements). We will focus on the use of visual and auditory information in order to build a model for anticipating the partner's gestures and their timing within the spoken interaction, possibly combined with a functional meaning of the gesture. Our goal is to investigate how auditive and visual modalities are used as communicative signals in various interactive situations, and how to learn interaction models which can ultimately be applied to develop natural human-robot interaction (cf. Beck et al., 2010, Jokinen et al. 2014).We are especially interested in time correlation between response token and head gestures, because it is known that recipient's nod usually co-occurs with response token in Japanese. A lot of previous studies attempted to predict some features of response token from precedent utterance to develop voice interactive system in Japanese. However, it is necessary to reveal, for instance the relationship between prosodic features of response token and the depth of nod, or the location of nod on the co-occurred response token in order to develop multimodal interactive system.

Finally, we plan for a comparison of the results using different corpora. It will be useful to compare various interactive situations and extract features that enable us to generalise over relevant attributes in interactive situations and also to explore methodological issues related to modelling and processing human physical characteristics.

6. Acknowledgement

We would like to thank all the participants who took part in the experiments as well as to our colleagues for their assistance in the preparation, collection, and post-processing of the data. This paper is based on results obtained from Future AI and Robot Technology Research and Development Project commissioned by the Japan New Energy and Industrial Technology Development Organization (NEDO).

7. References

Allwood, J., Cerrato, L., Jokinen, K., Navarretta C., Paggio,P.: The MUMIN Coding Scheme for the Annotation of Feedback, Turn Management and Sequencing Phenomena. Multimodal Corpora for Modelling Human Multimodal Behaviour. Special issue of the International Journal of Language Resources and Evaluation, 41(3-4), 273-287(2007). SpringerLink Online: http://www.springerlink.com/content/x745801041m525 53/fulltext.pdf

Baltrušaitis, T., Ahuja C., Morency, L.: Multimodal Machine Learning: A Survey and Taxonomy, in IEEE Transactions on Pattern Analysis and Machine Intelligence, vol. 41, no. 2, pp. 423-443, 1 Feb. 2019.

Beck, A., Canamero, L., Bard, K.A.: Towards an Affect Space for Robots to Display Emotional Body Language, in Proceedings of the 19th IEEEE International Symposium on Robot and Human Interactive Communication (Ro-MAN 2010), Principe di Piemonto -Viareggio, Italy, 2010.

Clark, H. H., Schaefer, E. F.: Collaborating on contributions to conversation. Language and Cognitive Processes, 2, 19-41 (1987).

Duncan, Jr., S.: Some signals and rules for taking speaking turns in conversations. Journal of Personality and Social Psychology, 23 (2), 283-292 (1972).

Endrass, B., Nakano, Y., Lipi, A. A., Rehm, M., André, E.: Culture-Related Topic Selection in Small Talk Conversations across Germany and Japan. Lecture Notes in Computer Science, 6895, 1-13 (2011).Feldman, R. S., Rim, B.: Fundamentals of Nonverbal Behavior. Cambridge: Cambridge University Press (1991).

Heimerl, A., Baur, T., Lingenfelser, F., Wagner, J., André, E.: NOVA - A tool for eXplainable Cooperative Machine Learning, in Proceedings of the 2019 8th International Conference on Affective Computing and Intelligent Interaction (ACII), Cambridge (2019).

Heylen, D., Krenn, B., Payr, S.: Companions, Virtual Butlers, Assistive Robots: Empirical and Theoretical Insights for Building Long-Term Social Relationships. In: Trappl, R. (ed.): Cybernetics and Systems 2010, pp. 539–570. Austrian Society for Cybernetic Studies. Vienna, Austria (2010).

Ijuin, K., Jokinen, K., Kato, T., Yamamoto, S.: Eye-gaze in social robot interactions – Grounding of information and eye-gaze patterns. JSAI 2019 (2019)

Jokinen, K.: Constructive Dialogue Modelling – Speech Interaction with Rational Agents. John Wiley & Sons, Chichester, UK (2009).

Jokinen, K.: Dialogue models for Social Robots. In: Proceedings of ICSR'2018, Qingdao, China (2018).

Jokinen, K.: The AICO corpus. Technical Report. AI Research Center, AIST. (2019).

Jokinen, K.: Pointing Gestures and Synchronous Communication Management. In: A. Esposito, N. Campbell, C. Vogel, A. Hussain, A. Nijholt, Eds., Development of Multimodal Interfaces: Active Listening and Synchrony, pp. 33-49. Berlin: Springer (2010)

Jokinen, K., Nishimura, S., Watanabe, K., Nishimura, T.: Human-Robot Dialogues for Explaining Activities. In: Proceedings of IWSDS-2018, Singapore (2018).

Jokinen, K., Wilcock, G.: Multimodal Open-Domain Conversations with the Nao Robot. In: Natural Interaction with Robots, Knowbots and Smartphones: Putting Spoken Dialogue Systems into Practice Springer, New York, pp. 213–224 (2014).

Kanda, T., Hirano, T., Eaton, D., Ishiguro, H.: Interactive robots as social partners and peer tutors for children: A field trial. Human-Computer Interaction, 19 (1), 61-84 (2004).

Kendon, A.: Gestures: Visible Action as Utterance. Cambridge: Cambridge University Press (2004).

Kita, S., Alibali, M. W., Chu, M.: How Do Gestures Influence Thinking and Speaking? The Gesture-for-Conceptualization Hypothesis. Psychological Review, 124(3), 245-266. (2017).

Lis, M., Navarretta C.: Classifying the form of iconic hand gestures from the linguistic categorization of co-occurring verbs. In: Proceedings of the European Symposium on Multimodal Communication (MMSym'13), Valetta, Malta (2014).

Maynard, S.: Japanese conversation: Self-contextualization through structure and interactional management. Norwood, NJ: Ablex (1989).

Navarretta, C., Ahlsén, E., Allwood, J., Jokinen, K., Paggio, P.: Feedback in Nordic First-Encounters: a Comparative Study. LREC 2012: 2494-2499

Navarretta, C., Ahlsen, E., Allwood, J., Jokinen, K., Paggio, P.: Feedback in Nordic firstencounters: a comparative study. Proceedings of 8th International Conference on Language Resources and Evaluation (LREC 2012), Istanbul, 2012.

Paggio, P., Navarretta, C.: Head movements, facial expressions and feedback in conversations: empirical evidence from Danish multimodal data. J. Multimodal User Interfaces 7(1-2): 29-37 (2013)

Ono, T., Imai, M., & Ishiguro, H. (2001). A Model of Embodied Communications with Gestures between Human and Robots. Proceedings of the Annual Meeting of the Cognitive Science Society, 23.

Senft, E., Baxter, P., Kennedy, J., Lemaignan, S., Belpaeme, T.: Supervised autonomy for online learning in human-robot interaction. Pattern Recognition Letters, 99: 77-86 (2017).

Sidner, C., Rich, C., Shayganfar, M., Bickmore, T., Ring, L. and Zhang, Z.: A Robotic Companion for Social Support of Isolated Older Adults. Procs of the 10th Annual ACM/IEEE International Conference on Human-Robot Interaction, 289-289 (2015).

Streeck, J.: Gesturecraft: The Manufacture of Meaning. Amsterdam: John Benjamins (2009).

Wilcock, G., Jokinen, K.: Advances in Wikipedia-based Interaction with Robots. ICMI Workshop Multi-modal, Multi-Party, Real-World Human-Robot Interaction, pp.13-18 (2014).

8. Appendix: AICO Annotation Scheme

8.1 Hand Gestures

8.1.1 Form

Hand gesture forms are classified into following 6 types based on the shape of a palm or fingers.

Up-open	Opening a palm upwards
Down-open	Opening a palm downwards
Sliced-open	Opening a palm sideways
Extended-finger	Extending a finger towards pointing
Curled-fingers	Curling fingers close to palm
Other	Gesture form not listed above

Table 2: Classification of hand gesture forms

8.1.2 Function

Hand gesture functions are classified into following 8 types in terms of communicative function.

Deictic	Pointing to a concrete or an abstract referent
Rhythmic	Giving rhythm to speech
Emphasis	Emphasising a particular point in talk
Iconic	Describing concrete or abstract objects
Emblem	Expressing a particular symbolic meaning that is culturally conditioned
Task	Performing a task
Adapter	Improving comfort or reducing stress
Other	Gesture function not listed above

Table 3: Classification of hand gesture functions

8.1.3 Trajectory

Hand gesture trajectory means the movement path of the gesturing hand. Those trajectries are classified into following 4 types.

Straight	Moving up, down or sideways
Complex	Complex directions
Static	Staying in the same position and location
Touch	Like static but keep touching

Table 4: Classification of hand gesture trajectories

8.1.4 Handedness

Handedness is decided based on whether the gesture is performed with one or both hands.

Both	Both hands
Single	Single hand

Table 5: Classification of handedness

8.1.5 Repetition

Hand gesture repetition means whether the gesture is composed of a single movement or several similar movements.

Single	Single movement
Repeated	Repeated movements

Table 6: Classification of hand gesture repetition

8.2 Head Gestures

8.2.1 Form

Head gesture forms are cassified into following 6 types based on the movements of the gesturing head.

Jerk	Moving sudden up
Nod	Moving up-down
Shake	Rotating side-to-side
Tilt	Tilting on one side
Waggle	Moving sideways
Other	Gesture form not listed above

Table 7: Classification of head gesture forms

8.2.2 Function

Head gesture functions are classified into following 7 types in terms of communicative function.

Acknowledge	Giving encouraging feedback to the partner
NonAccept	Objecting or withdrawing from what the partner is saying or doing
Emphasis	Emphasising some particular point in talk
Turn	Giving turn to the partner or accepting turn from the partner
Adapter	improving comfort or reducing stress
Elicit	Eliciting feedback from the partner
Other	Head function not listed above

Table 8: Classification of hand gesture functions

8.2.3 Repetition

Head gesture repetition means whether the gesture is composed of a single movement or several similar movements.

Single	Single movement
Repeated	Repeated movements

Table 9: Classification of hand gesture repetition

8.3 Body Gestures

8.3.1 Form

Body gesture forms are cassified into following 3 types based on the movements of the gesturing body.

Forward	Leaning towards the partner
Backward	Leaning away from the partner
Other	Gesture form not listed above

Table 10: Classification of body gesture forms

8.3.2 Function

Body gesture functions are classified into following 8 types in terms of communicative function.

Interest	Giving feedback that shows interest to the partner's talk
BetterContact	Moving closer to hear or speak clearly to the partner
NonAccept	Objecting or withdrawing oneself from what the partner is saying or doing
Emphasis	Emphasising some particular point in talk
Turn	Giving turn to the partner, or accepting turn
Emblem	Expressing a particular symbolic meaning that is culturally conditioned
Adapter	Improving comfort or reducing stress
Other	Body gesture function not listed above

Table 11: Classification of hand gesture functions

8.3.3 Repetition

Body gesture repetition means whether the gesture is composed of a brief single movement, a long single movement or several similar movements.

Single	Single movement
Repeated	Repeated movements
Static	Staying in the same position and location for few second

Table 12: Classification of hand gesture repetition

Proceedings of ONION 2020: Workshop on peOple in laNguage, vIsiOn and the miNd, pages 15–21
Language Resources and Evaluation Conference (LREC 2020), Marseille, 11–16 May 2020

Automatic Detection and Classification of Head Movements in Face-to-Face Conversations

Patrizia Paggio[1,2], Manex Agirrezabal[1], Bart Jongejan[1], Costanza Navarretta[1]
[1]University of Copenhagen, [2]University of Malta
paggio@hum.ku.dk, manex.aguirrezabal@hum.ku.dk, bartj@hum.ku.dk, costanza@hum.ku.dk

Abstract

This paper presents an approach to automatic head movement detection and classification in data from a corpus of video-recorded face-to-face conversations in Danish involving 12 different speakers. A number of classifiers were trained with different combinations of visual, acoustic and word features and tested in a leave-one-out cross validation scenario. The visual movement features were extracted from the raw video data using OpenPose, the acoustic ones from the sound files using Praat, and the word features from the transcriptions. The best results were obtained by a Multilayer Perceptron classifier, which reached an average 0.68 F1 score across the 12 speakers for head movement detection, and 0.40 for head movement classification given four different classes. In both cases, the classifier outperformed a simple most frequent class baseline, a more advanced baseline only relying on velocity features, and linear classifiers using different combinations of features.

Keywords: head movement detection, multimodal corpora, visual and speech features

1. Introduction

Head movements play an important role in face-to-face communication in that they provide an effective means to express and elicit feedback, and consequently establish grounding and rapport between speakers; they contribute to turn exchange; they are used by speakers to manage their own communicative behaviour, e.g. in connection with lexical search (Allwood, 1988; Yngve, 1970; Duncan, 1972; McClave, 2000). Therefore, it is crucial for conversational systems to be able to identify and interpret speakers' head movements as well as generate them correctly when interacting with users (Ruttkay and Pelachaud, 2006).

This paper is a contribution to the automatic identification of head movements from raw video data coming from face-to-face dyadic conversations. It builds on previous work where a number of models were trained to detect head movements based on movement and speech features, and extends that work in several directions by extracting movement features using newer software, by trying to distinguish between different kinds of movement, and by training and testing speaker-independent models based on a larger dataset.

The paper is structured as follows. In section 2 we discuss related work in the area. Section 3 is dedicated to the features for the prediction of head movements. In section 4 we present the corpus that we used for the current study. Finally in section 5 we discuss the results and propose some possible future directions.

2. Related work

Several studies have been relatively successful in performing head movement detection from tracked data, for example by using coordinates obtained through eye-tracking (Kapoor and Picard, 2001; Tan and Rong, 2003) or Kinect sensors (Wei et al., 2013). A different approach to the task is to detect head movements in raw video data. Such an approach has the potential of making available large amount of data to train systems to deal with multimodal communication in different languages and communicative scenarios. Large annotated multimodal corpora are in turn a prerequisite to the development of natural multimodal interactive systems. Surveys of the way computer vision techniques can be applied to gesture recognition are given in Wu and Huang (1999) and Gavrila (1999). Both works conclude, however, that the field is still a fairly new one, and many problems remain as yet unsolved.

Work has also been done trying to detect gestures based on visual as well as language or speech features. In this line of research, Morency et al. (2005) proposed a methodology where SVM and HMM models were trained to predict feedback nods and shakes in human-robot interactions. The visual features used for head movement recognition were enriched with features from the dialogue context. It can be argued, however, that human-robot interaction is much more constrained than spontaneous human dialogue, and thus the task of predicting the user's head movements is probably easier, or at least different than in human-human communication data. In Morency et al. (2007), models were trained to recognise head movements in video frames in a variety of datasets based on visual features obtained from tracked head velocities or eye gaze estimates extracted from video data. A number of different models were compared in the study, and it was found that LDCRF (Latent-Dynamic Conditional Random Field) was the best performing of the models. The authors attribute the result to the fact that the model is good at dealing with unsegmented sequences, in this case movement sequences. Morency (2009) studied the co-occurrence between head gestures and speech cues such as specific words and pauses in multi-party conversations, and relevant contextual cues were used to improve a vision-based LDCRF head gesture recognition model.

In Jongejan (2012), OpenCV was applied to the detection of head movement from videos based on velocity and acceleration, in combination with customisable thresholds, for the automatic annotation of head movements using the ANVIL tool (Kipp, 2004). The obtained annotations correlated well with the manual annotation at the onset, but generated a high number of false positives. In Jongejan et al. (2017), three visual movement features were used to train an SVM classifier of head movement.

Frid et al. (2017) used the corpus of read news in Swedish described in Ambrazaitis and House (2017) to detect head movements that co-occur with words. The head movements were manually annotated and OpenCV for frontal face detection was used in order to calculate velocity and acceleration features. A Xgboost classifier was trained to predict absence or presence of head movements co-occurring with words.

Acoustic features have also been used for head movement prediction. For example Germesin and Wilson (2009) combined pitch and energy of voice with word, pause and head pose information to identify agreement and disagreement signals in meeting data. Such work is based on linguistic and psycho-linguistic findings that have shown a tight relationship between facial movements and acoustic prominence, to the point of talking about audiovisual prominence (Granström and House, 2005; Swerts and Krahmer, 2008; Ambrazaitis and House, 2017).

In the work by Paggio et al. (2018), movement features were considered together with acoustic features to identify head movements in conversational data. The authors performed several experiments with different feature sets and also, several prediction paradigms were tested, including common classifiers and sequence-based models. It was observed that a Multilayer Perceptron showed the best results when trained on one speaker and tested on another one. In this study, we build on those preliminary results by extending our dataset to consider twelve different speakers, and we experiment with the classification of different head movement types.

3. Predictive features

Similarly to what was done in Paggio et al. (2018), three time-related derivatives with respect to the changing position of the head are used here as features for the identification of head movements: *velocity*, *acceleration* and *jerk*. Velocity is change of position per unit of time, acceleration is change of velocity per unit of time, and finally jerk is change of acceleration per unit of time. We suggest that a sequence of frames for which jerk has a high value either horizontally or vertically may correspond to the *stroke* of the movement (Kendon, 2004).

OpenPose (Cao et al., 2018) was used to extract nose tip positions from the data. Using a sliding window, velocity, acceleration and jerk values were computed for video frame sequences using a polynomial (linear, quadratic and cubic, respectively) regression over a number of observations of nose tip positions. Several window frames were experimented with. The results reported in this paper were obtained by considering 9 frames for velocity, 11 for acceleration and 13 for jerk. For each of the three derivatives, four values are computed for each frame and used to train the models. The 12 values are both the cartesian (x and y) and polar (radius and angle) coordinates of the velocity, acceleration and jerk vectors. Since we analyse video data, we do not have depth information, and so we are restricted to express velocity, acceleration and jerk as vectors in a two dimensional plane. Angle values have integer values between 1 and 12, like the directions on a clock dial.

It must be noted that the video recordings are characterised by 25 frames per second and a resolution of either 640x360 (.avi) or 640x369 (.mov). Thus the quality is quite low given today's standards. In addition, since the participants are recorded almost in full height, the head movements are very tiny when expressed in pixels. All of this is bound to have an effect on how accurately the movement derivatives can predict head movement.

Acoustic features were extracted from the speech channels of all speakers using the PRAAT software (Boersma and Weenink, 2009). In general, several studies indicate that head movements are likely to occur together with prosodic stress, whereas the opposite is not necessarily true (Hadar et al., 1983; Loehr, 2007). Since in Danish, which is the language of our study, stress is expressed through fundamental frequency, vowel duration and quality, as well as intensity (Thorsen, 1980), we decided to rely on pitch and intensity features to model a possible relation between focal patterns and head movements. F0 values and intensity values were sampled with 25 frames per second as is done for the movement features and added to the training data. The hypothesis is that changes in pitch or peaks of intensity might be associated with head movement strokes, and thus help in identifying movement.

Based on the analysis of co-occurrence patterns between head movements and verbalisation in the corpus data (Paggio et al., 2017), we finally added to the predictive features information as to whether the person performing the movement, the *gesturer*, is speaking or not. This binary feature was added to each frame based on the speech transcription, which was done manually and includes word boundaries.

4. Data, training and test setup

Figure 1: Screen shot from one of the video recordings showing combined almost frontal camera views

The data used for this study is taken from the Danish NOMCO corpus (Paggio et al., 2010), a collection of twelve video-recorded first encounter conversations between pairs of speakers (half females, half males) for a total interaction of approximately one hour. Each speaker took part in two different conversations, one with a male and one with a female. The speakers are standing in front of each other. The conversations were recorded in a studio using three different cameras and two cardioid microphones. For the work presented here we used a version of the recordings in which both speakers are being viewed almost frontally, and the two views are combined in a singled video as shown in Figure 1. The data have been annotated

Movement type	No. movements	No. frames
None	NA	125,747
Nod	926	21,755
Shake	337	9,505
Other	1,854	41,053
Total movement	3,117	72,313

Table 1: Different types of head movements in the dataset: total number of frames and whole movements

	None	Nod	Shake	Other	All
Mean	10,479	1,813	792	3,421	6,026
CV	0.13	0.47	0.50	0.20	0.20

Table 2: Distribution of different head movement types in the dataset: average mean number of frames and coefficient of variation across 12 speakers

with many different annotation layers (Paggio and Navarretta, 2016), including a manually obtained speech transcription with word-specific boundaries, and temporal segments corresponding to different types of head movement (Allwood et al., 2007). The Cohen's (1960) κ score results of inter-coder agreement experiments involving two annotators are between 0.72 and 0.8 for the identification and classification of head movements (Navarretta et al., 2011). For this study, we have focused on two ways of looking at the head movements; i. distinguishing between head movement and absence of it; ii. distinguishing between nods, shakes, other kind of head movement, and no movement.

In table 1 we show the distribution of the four types of head movement in the annotated corpus both in terms of entire movement sequences and number of video frames. Thus, 3,117 head movements were annotated in total, corresponding to 72,313 movement frames. Frames containing no head movement constitute by far the majority of the video footage. The *Nod* class subsumes both down and up nods. It was singled out together with *Shake* because these two classes have been targeted previously in head movement detection studies (Morency et al., 2005). The *Other* category groups a number of distinct types in the annotation, i.e. *HeadBackward, HeadForward, SideTurn, Tilt, Waggle* and *HeadOther*.

There is of course speaker-dependent variation in the frequency of the various movement types. Table 2 displays mean averages and coefficient of variations for how different movement and non movement frames are distributed across the twelve speakers. The figures show that the frequency of occurrence of both *Nod* and *Shake* varies considerably in the speaker sample.

The duration of the head movements in the annotated corpus is 934.78 ms on average (SD: 579.44 ms). A histogram of head movement duration is given in Figure 2. Although most movements are shorter than 1500 ms, we see a long tail of outliers with a maximum duration of up to 7,080 ms.

To derive training data from the twelve annotated videos, movement, acoustic and word features were extracted as explained in the previous section so that for each frame in each video a vector was created with features expressing presence/absence of movement, a label for each of the four movement classes, four velocity, four acceleration and

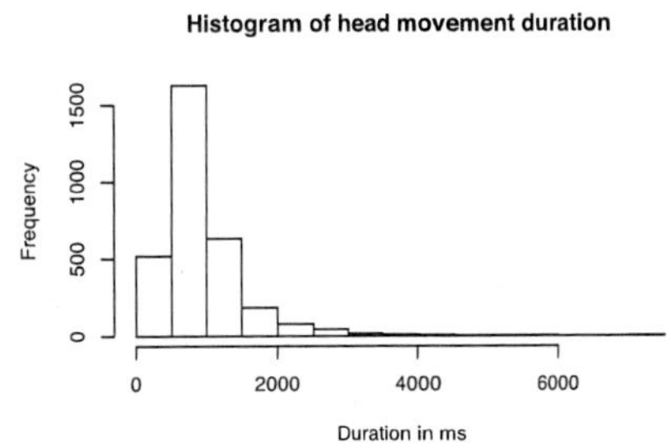

Figure 2: Duration of annotated head movements in the dataset

four jerk features, pitch and intensity values referring to the gesturer and a binary feature expressing whether the same gesturer is speaking or not.

The data were then used to train a number of different classifiers to predict the head movements of each speaker given training data from the other eleven speakers (leave-one-out cross validation). In what follows, we will report accuracy and F1 results achieved by the various classifiers on average across speakers. It should be kept in mind, however, that there is variation across speakers in number of types of head movement produced, as already noted. Moreover, the accuracy of the classifiers may be influenced by the fact that some speakers are sometimes situated on the left and sometimes on the right, and others are in the same position in both the conversations they took part in.

As mentioned earlier, two tasks were conducted. The first is detection of head movement (irrespective of the type), and the second is classification of head movement type given the four classes *None, Nod, Shake* and *Other*.

Two baselines were chosen. The first one corresponds to the results obtained by a simple most-frequent category model, which will always predict that there is no movement in the frame. The second one is a logistic regression classifier that only uses velocity features. We then experimented with the complete range of movement derivatives (velocity, acceleration and jerk). Finally, we added acoustic and word information relative to the gesturer. The following classifier types were used to train models using the various feature combinations: i. a Logistic Regression (LR) classifier, which is an example of a simple model, ii. a linear Support Vector Machine (LINEARSVC), which was used by several earlier studies for head movement detection, and iii. a Multilayer Perceptron (MLP) with four layers, as an example of a non-linear classifier.[1]

5. Results

The results of the binary classification experiments are given in terms of average accuracy in table 3 and F1 score (macro average) in table 4. Looking at accuracy first, all models perform better than the most frequent class (MF)

[1]The data and the Jupyter notebooks that were used in our experiments can be found at `https://github.com/kuhumcst/head_movement_detection`.

Exp	Features	MF	LR	LINEARSVC	MLP
1	Only velocity	0.635	0.686	0.680	0.707
2	All visual features (no sound)	0.635	0.721	0.718	**0.733**
3	All visual and acoustic (only gesturer)	0.635	0.722	0.718	0.730
4	All visual and acoustic+word (only gesturer)	0.635	0.725	0.723	0.730

Table 3: Accuracy results of classification experiments (mean over 12 speakers). Classes are presence and absence of movement.

Exp	Features	MF	LR	LINEARSVC	MLP
1	Only velocity	0.387	0.575	0.557	0.648
2	All visual features (no sound)	0.387	0.644	0.633	0.684
3	All visual and acoustic (only gesturer)	0.387	0.646	0.634	0.681
4	All visual and acoustic+word (only gesturer)	0.387	0.658	0.650	**0.684**

Table 4: F1 results (macro average) of classification experiments (mean over 12 speakers). Classes are presence and absence of movement.

		Predicted as				
		None	Nod	Shake	Other	Sum
Gold value	None	**113,566**	1,984	327	9,870	125,747
	Nod	13,429	**4,528**	74	3,724	21,755
	Shake	5,977	184	**618**	2,726	9,505
	Other	23,148	2,089	584	**15,232**	41,053

Table 5: Classification of different types of head movements in the whole dataset: error matrix

Movement type	No. frames	Precision (%)	Recall (%)
None	125,747	72.74	90.31
Nod	21,755	51.54	20.81
Shake	9,505	38.55	6.5
Other	41,053	48.28	37.1

Table 6: Classification of different types of head movements in the whole dataset: total number of frames, precision and recall for each type

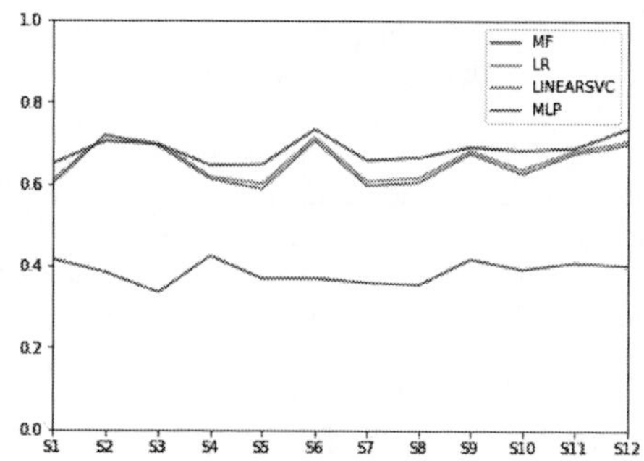

Figure 3: Visualisation of the F1-score of the binary model that include all features (exp. 4 in table 4)

baseline. We also see that the MLP classifier performs better than all the others irrespective of the combination of features used in the training. The overall best accuracy is achieved by MLP using all the three movement features, whereas acoustic and word features seem to introduce some noise (even though the difference between the MLP results in experiment 2 on the one hand and 2 and 3 on the other is marginal).

Turning to F1, we observe again that all models definitely outperform the baseline, and that the MLP classifier is consistently the best in all experiments. In this case, the best result is achieved either using the entire range of features or only the visual ones. Adding acoustic features alone produces a slightly lower F1.

Figure 3 shows how the F1 score obtained by the best binary models, i.e. those trained with the complete range of features, varies depending on the speaker. The MLP classifier is not only the best performing one on average, but also the one where the F1 score varies the least. However, there is still some variation. In fact, the standard deviation for the results achieved by MLP is 0.053 for accuracy and 0.046 for F1.

We now turn to the results of the multi-class prediction experiments, which are shown in table 7 for accuracy and table 8 for F1 score (macro average). Determining the type of head movement in a multi-class prediction scenario is a more difficult task than having to choose between movement and non-movement. Therefore, it is not surprising that the results are generally worse. Nevertheless, all the models perform better than the baseline both as regards accuracy and F1. Also in this case, MLP is generally the best classifier. If we now focus on the accuracy results first, we see again that the best accuracy is achieved by MLP when using all the movement features but no acoustic or word features. When we look at the F1 scores, however, we see that acoustic features this time not only help the classifier, but provide the best performing model in combination with movement features.

Further analysis of the results is provided by the error matrix in table 5, which relates to the best performing classifier (MLP in exp. 3). We see first of all that head movements of all types are confused with no movement, and to some extent with movements of type *Other*. Nods and shakes, on the contrary, are seldom exchanged for one another, which seems a good result given the fact that they are quite different from the point of view of their movement characteristics.

In table 6 we show precision and recall figures for the different movement types. Recall is in general low for movement frames, while precision is better. We see this as an advantage in that an automatic procedure that misses exist-

Exp	Features	MF	LR	LINEARSVC	MLP
1	Only velocity	0.635	0.648	0.646	0.657
2	All visual features (no sound)	0.635	0.660	0.657	**0.677**
3	All visual and acoustic (only gesturer)	0.635	0.661	0.658	0.676
4	All visual and acoustic+word (only gesturer)	0.635	0.668	0.665	0.679

Table 7: Accuracy results of multi-class prediction experiments (mean over 12 speakers). Classes are nod, shake, other, none.

Exp	Features	MF	LR	LINEARSVC	MLP
1	Only velocity	0.194	0.256	0.249	0.308
2	All visual features (no sound)	0.194	0.291	0.277	0.396
3	All visual and acoustic (only gesturer)	0.194	0.294	0.279	**0.397**
4	All visual and acoustic+word (only gesturer)	0.194	0.313	0.297	0.394

Table 8: F1 results (macro average) of multi-class prediction experiments (mean over 12 speakers). Classes are nod, shake, other, none.

ing head movements seems more acceptable than one that finds non-existing ones. Precision in the detection of head movements is highest for *Nod*, followed by *Other*, followed by *Shake*. The degree of precision depends not only on frequency of occurrence (there are more nods than shakes), but also on how homogeneous the classes are (the class *Other* is not as homogeneous as the class *Nod*).

6. Discussion

In general, it is difficult to compare our results directly to what other head movement detection studies have achieved because of the diversity of recording settings, number of participants, communicative situations etc. The work that resembles ours the most in terms of the methodology used is perhaps the paper by Frid et al. (2017) in that they also rely on movement derivatives. They also look at the co-occurrence of head movements and words, but do so in a different way by predicting for each word whether it is accompanied by a movement or not. Their results, 0.89 accuracy and 0.61 F1 score, are not very dissimilar from those obtained by our best model in the binary classification.

It must be noted, however, that we are detecting head movements in less favourable conditions since our subjects are recorded in full body size. In addition, the quality of our videos is, as already mentioned, not up to today's standards. Furthermore, the acoustic signal is also far from optimal because the microphones were hanging from the ceiling rather than being close to the participants' mouths.

The present study is a further development of the earlier experiment reported in Paggio et al. (2018), where we performed head movement detection in a subset of the data only consisting of two speakers. The best result was obtained in that study by a Multilayer Perceptron trained on visual and acoustic features, which achieved 0.75 accuracy and outperformed a classifier trained on monomodal visual features. The performance of the best model in the current study, which applies to the entire dataset, is only about 2% lower, thus showing that our methodology is reasonably robust.

An interesting question is whether approaching the problem in terms of single frames is a good way of approximating what the human annotators did. After all, they were asked to annotate whole head movements, not individual frames.

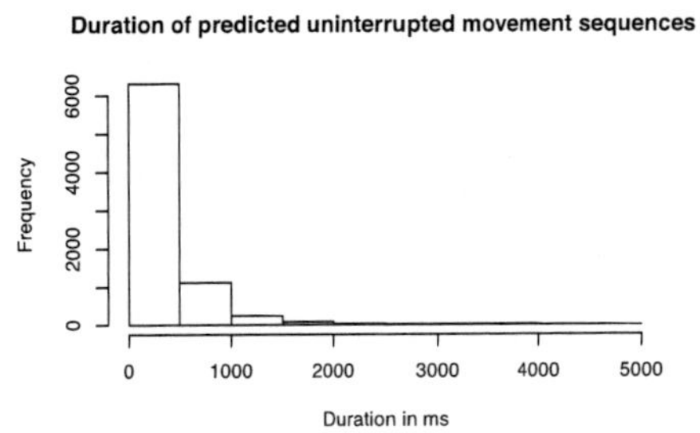

Figure 4: Histogram of the duration of uninterrupted sequences of movement frames predicted by the binary MLP classifier in exp. 4

A way to compare the results of the frame-wise predictions made by the models is to look at the number and duration of uninterrupted movement frame sequences and compare them with the gold standard. The total number of movements predicted by the best binary classifier is 7,782, and their mean duration is 291.25 ms (SD: 360.91). In comparison to the annotated movements, the classifier detects many more but shorter ones. In figure 4 we visualise the whole distribution of the duration of the predicted movements. If we compare it with the histogram in figure 2, we can clearly see that the classifier tends to find many more shorter movements (up to 500 ms), and even though the distribution is also left-skewed, the maximum duration of 4,880 is considerably shorter than the longest movement in the gold standard. There may be several explanations for these differences, e.g. the fact that annotators may have seen a sequence of movements as an uninterrupted repeated gesture of a certain kind rather than separate individual ones.

Looking at the feature combinations used in the experiments, the results confirm the fact that combining the three movement derivatives in the training reliably improves detection and classification for all the models. It can be discussed, however, whether all the values currently used in the vectors are in fact necessary. Having a representation of velocity, acceleration and jerk not only in terms of polar coordinates but also in terms of cartesian coordinates is redundant since such representations are equivalent. We repeated some of the experiments without the inclusion of polar coordinates. Only the MLP classifier was not adversely influenced by this and became even marginally better. The linear classifiers, on the other hand, performed not any better than the baseline without the polar coordinates.

The role played by the acoustic and word features, on the contrary, is not totally clear in that they only add marginal gains to the F1 scores obtained by the models and in some cases even harm them. It is possible that the speech signal is superfluous, but also that we have not found the most efficient way to combine those features with the visual ones. More research is needed to understand this.

Finally, as we noted the performance of the classifiers varies depending on the speaker. A first analysis of the data indicates that the factors which might influence the results in this direction are the types of head movement performed by the speakers as well as whether the speaker is standing on the same side during the two conversations or not.

7. Conclusions and future work

In conclusion, we have shown that head movements can be detected in unseen speaker data by an MLP classifier trained with multimodal data including movement and acoustic features. The results achieved by this classifier perform at state-of-the-art level. When the same method is applied to the classification of four different types of head movement in the same data, the performance decreases.

In order to develop the present work further, we can investigate different approaches. Firstly, we plan to add more features from OpenPose: the position of ears and chin, for example, might be helpful to add to the position of the nose for some of the head movements. An alternative to OpenPose, or a method that we would like to use in combination with it, could be found in computer vision techniques that identify changing head positions as proposed in Ruiz et al. (2018), who trained a multiloss Convolutional Neural Network on a synthetically created dataset in order to predict yaw, pitch and roll from image intensities.

Secondly, we intend to investigate different ways to use acoustic and word features, either by adding more features or by using them in more selective ways for specific head movement classes.

Thirdly, we would like to analyse the extent to which the depth of the neural network contributes to the results by testing different numbers of layers. Furthermore, we would like to experiment with sequential models such as Recurrent Neural Networks (RNN), which are often used to analyse video sequences and might therefore predict gestures more precisely than the classifiers we have tested until now. In that connection, it would also be interesting to experiment with an architecture in which representations are learnt separately for each feature by different networks and then concatenated into one vector.

Finally, we want to carry out a more precise comparison of the movements predicted and the annotated ones by making the predictions readable by the ANVIL gesture annotation tool.

8. Ethical considerations

We have obtained written permission by the participants to use the videos for research purposes specific to the project within which the recordings were obtained. Therefore, we are making all the features extracted from the corpus available together with the code we have used to train and test the classifiers. However, we do not share the videos or the transcriptions from the corpus because of privacy and data protection issues.

9. References

Allwood, J., Cerrato, L., Jokinen, K., Navarretta, C., and Paggio, P. (2007). The MUMIN coding scheme for the annotation of feedback, turn management and sequencing phenomena. In Jean-Claude Martin, et al., editors, *Multimodal Corpora for Modelling Human Multimodal Behaviour*, volume 41 of *Special issue of the International Journal of Language Resources and Evaluation*, pages 273–287. Springer.

Allwood, J. (1988). The Structure of Dialog. In Martin M. Taylor, et al., editors, *Structure of Multimodal Dialog II*, pages 3–24. John Benjamins, Amsterdam.

Ambrazaitis, G. and House, D. (2017). Acoustic features of multimodal prominences: Do visual beat gestures affect verbal pitch accent realization? In Slim Ouni, et al., editors, *Proceedings of The 14th International Conference on Auditory-Visual Speech Processing (AVSP2017)*. KTH.

Boersma, P. and Weenink, D. (2009). Praat: doing phonetics by computer (version 5.1.05) [computer program]. Retrieved May 1, 2009, from http://www.praat.org/.

Cao, Z., Hidalgo, G., Simon, T., Wei, S.-E., and Sheikh, Y. (2018). OpenPose: realtime multi-person 2D pose estimation using Part Affinity Fields. In *arXiv preprint arXiv:1812.08008*.

Cohen, J. (1960). A coefficient of agreement for nominal scales. *Educational and Psychological Measurement*, 20(1):37–46.

Duncan, S. (1972). Some signals and rules for taking speaking turns in conversations. *Journal of Personality and Social Psychology*, 23:283–292.

Frid, J., Ambrazaitis, G., Svensson-Lundmark, M., and House, D. (2017). Towards classification of head movements in audiovisual recordings of read news. In *Proceedings of the 4th European and 7th Nordic Symposium on Multimodal Communication (MMSYM 2016)*, number 141, pages 4–9, Copenhagen, September 2016. Linköping University Electronic Press, Linköpings universitet.

Gavrila, D. (1999). The visual analysis of human movement: A survey. *Computer Vision and Image Understanding*, 73(1):82 – 98.

Germesin, S. and Wilson, T. (2009). Agreement detection in multiparty conversation. In *Proceedings of ICMI-MLMI 2009*, pages 7–14.

Granström, B. and House, D. (2005). Audiovisual representation of prosody in expressive speech communication. *Speech Communication*, 46(3):473–484, July.

Hadar, U., Steiner, T., Grant, E., and Clifford Rose, F. (1983). Head Movement Correlates of Juncture and Stress at Sentence Level. *Language and Speech*, 26(2):117–129, April.

Jongejan, B., Paggio, P., and Navarretta, C. (2017). Classifying head movements in video-recorded conversations based on movement velocity, acceleration and jerk. In *Proceedings of the 4th European and 7th Nordic Symposium on Multimodal Communication (MMSYM 2016), Copenhagen, 29-30 September 2016*, number 141, pages 10–17. Linköping University Electronic Press, Linköpings universitet.

Jongejan, B. (2012). Automatic annotation of head velocity and acceleration in Anvil. In *Proceedings of the Eighth International Conference on Language Resources and Evaluation (LREC'12)*, pages 201–208. European Language Resources Distribution Agency.

Kapoor, A. and Picard, R. W. (2001). A real-time head nod and shake detector. In *Proceedings of the 2001 Workshop on Perceptive User Interfaces*, PUI '01, pages 1–5, New York, NY, USA. ACM.

Kendon, A. (2004). *Gesture*. Cambridge University Press.

Kipp, M. (2004). *Gesture Generation by Imitation – From Human Behavior to Computer Character Animation*. Boca Raton, Florida: Dissertation.com.

Loehr, D. P. (2007). Aspects of rhythm in gesture and speech. *Gesture*, 7(2).

McClave, E. (2000). Linguistic functions of head movements in the context of speech. *Journal of Pragmatics*, 32:855–878.

Morency, L.-P., Sidner, C., Lee, C., and Darrell, T. (2005). Contextual recognition of head gestures. In *Proc. Int. Conf. on Multimodal Interfaces (ICMI)*.

Morency, L.-P., Quattoni, A., and Darrell, T. (2007). Latent-dynamic discriminative models for continuous gesture recognition. In *2007 IEEE conference on computer vision and pattern recognition*, pages 1–8. IEEE.

Morency, L.-P. (2009). Co-occurrence graphs: contextual representation for head gesture recognition during multiparty interactions. In *Proceedings of the Workshop on Use of Context in Vision Processing*, pages 1–6.

Navarretta, C., Ahlsén, E., Allwood, J., Jokinen, K., and Paggio, P. (2011). Creating Comparable Multimodal Corpora for Nordic Languages. In *Proceedings of the 18th Conference Nordic Conference of Computational Linguistics*, pages 153–160, Riga, Latvia, May 11-13.

Paggio, P. and Navarretta, C. (2016). The Danish NOMCO corpus: Multimodal interaction in first acquaintance conversations. *Language Resources and Evaluation*, pages 1–32.

Paggio, P., Allwood, J., Ahlsén, E., Jokinen, K., and Navarretta, C. (2010). The NOMCO multimodal nordic resource - goals and characteristics. In *Proceedings of the Seventh conference on International Language Resources and Evaluation (LREC'10)*, Valletta, Malta. European Language Resources Association (ELRA).

Paggio, P., Navarretta, C., and Jongejan, B. (2017). Automatic identification of head movements in video-recorded conversations: Can words help? In *Proceedings of the Sixth Workshop on Vision and Language*, pages 40–42, Valencia, Spain, April. Association for Computational Linguistics.

Paggio, P., Jongejan, B., Agirrezabal, M., and Navarretta, C. (2018). Detecting head movements in video-recorded dyadic conversations. In *Proceedings of the 20th International Conference on Multimodal Interaction: Adjunct*, pages 1–6.

Ruiz, N., Chong, E., and Rehg, J. (2018). Fine-grained head pose estimation without keypoints. In *Proceedings of the IEEE Conference on Computer Vision and Pattern Recognition Workshops*, pages 2074–2083.

Ruttkay, Z. and Pelachaud, C. (2006). *From Brows to Trust: Evaluating Embodied Conversational Agents*. Human–Computer Interaction Series. Springer Netherlands.

Swerts, M. and Krahmer, E. (2008). Facial expression and prosodic prominence: Effects of modality and facial area. *Journal of Phonetics*, 36(2):219–238.

Tan, W. and Rong, G. (2003). A real-time head nod and shake detector using HMMs. *Expert Systems with Applications*, 25(3):461–466.

Thorsen, N. (1980). Neutral stress, emphatic stress, and sentence Intonation in Advanced Standard Copenhagen Danish. Technical Report 14, University of Copenhagen.

Wei, H., Scanlon, P., Li, Y., Monaghan, D. S., and O'Connor, N. E. (2013). Real-time head nod and shake detection for continuous human affect recognition. In *14th International Workshop on Image Analysis for Multimedia Interactive Services (WIAMIS)*, pages 1–4. IEEE.

Wu, Y. and Huang, T. S. (1999). Vision-based gesture recognition: A review. In *International Gesture Workshop*, pages 103–115. Springer.

Yngve, V. (1970). On getting a word in edgewise. In *Papers from the sixth regional meeting of the Chicago Linguistic Society*, pages 567–578.

Proceedings of ONION 2020: Workshop on peOple in laNguage, vIsiOn and the miNd, pages 22–27
Language Resources and Evaluation Conference (LREC 2020), Marseille, 11–16 May 2020

"You move THIS!": Annotation of Pointing Gestures on Tabletop Interfaces in Low Awareness Situations

Dimitra Anastasiou, Hoorieh Afkari, Valérie Maquil
Luxembourg Institute of Science and Technology (LIST)
IT for Innovative Services (ITIS) Department
5, avenue des Hauts Fourneaux L-4362 Esch/Alzette, Luxembourg
{dimitra.anastasiou, hoorieh.afkari, valerie.maquil}@list.lu

Abstract

This paper analyses pointing gestures during low awareness situations occurring in a collaborative problem-solving activity implemented on an interactive tabletop interface. Awareness is considered as crucial requirement to support fluid and natural collaboration. We focus on pointing gestures as strategy to maintain awareness. We describe the results from a user study with five groups, each group consisting of three participants, who were asked to solve a task collaboratively on a tabletop interface. The ideal problem-solving solution would have been, if the three participants had been fully aware of what their personal area is depicting and had communicated this properly to the peers. However, often some participants are hesitant due to lack of awareness, some other want to take the lead work or expedite the process, and therefore pointing gestures to others' personal areas arise. Our results from analyzing a multimodal corpus of 168.68 minutes showed that in 95% of the cases, one user pointed to the personal area of the other, while in a few cases (3%) a user not only pointed, but also performed a touch gesture on the personal area of another user. In our study, the *mean* for such pointing gestures in low awareness situations per minute and for all groups was *M=1.96, SD=0.58.*

Keywords: awareness, collaborative problem-solving, interactive tabletops, pointing gestures, user study

1. Introduction

Collaborative problem-solving (ColPS) is included in the Learning and Innovation skills of the 21st Century. It is defined as "the abilities to recognize the points of view of other persons in a group; contribute knowledge, experience, and expertise in a constructive way; identify the need for contributions and how to manage them; recognize structure and procedure involved in resolving a problem; and as a member of the group, build and develop group knowledge and understanding" (Griffin et al., 2012). ColPS represents the interaction of two distinct, though tightly connected dimensions of skills: i) *complex problem-solving* as the cognitive dimension and ii) *collaboration* as the interpersonal dimension (OECD, 2017).

During collaborative activities, awareness is considered as crucial. It can reduce effort, increase efficiency, and reduce errors (Gutwin & Greenberg, 2002).

In this paper, we focus on pointing gestures that are performed to reestablish awareness during collaborative problem-solving using a tangible tabletop interface. Our research question is whether and how are pointing gestures related to "low awareness" situations. We describe a between-group user study with five groups of three participants each, who were asked to solve a problem collaboratively. This collaborative problem is a computer-simulated scenario about an imaginary planet; the participants need to act as space mining crew in order to mine valuable minerals and ship them to earth. The main task of the participants is to collaboratively locate and mine the requested minerals meanwhile avoiding the threats of the environment in the shared activity area. Information and controls were split in three personal areas, each of them dedicated to one participant with the aim to give different and complementary responsibilities to each of the participants.

The ideal problem-solving solution would be that each user first fully understands the information and features of their own personal area, then reflects this understanding when communicating to the peers and last, takes action (i.e. manipulating the buttons) after having agreed to suggestions of their peers. However, we noticed that users often instructed each other about which buttons to press, making use of co-speech communicative gestures.

In this paper, we focus on pointing gesture cases used in these situations. More precisely, we are interested in the use of pointing gestures towards other users' personal areas with the intention to obtain and maintain awareness in collaborative problem-solving situations. Therefore, the goal of this paper is the gesture data analysis of a multimodal corpus as resulted by a study on collaborative problem-solving using a tabletop.

This paper is laid out as follows: in Section 2 we present related work with regards to awareness, interference, and collaboration on tabletop interfaces. In Section 3 we present our research goal along with a few examples of low awareness situations that we observed in our user study. Our study design is presented in Section 4 together with the computer-simulated problem. In Section 5 we present the main contribution of this paper, our multimodal corpus and its data analysis. We close this paper with a discussion and future work in Section 6.

2. Related Work

Our research work is in the domain of collaborative problem-solving on interactive tabletop interfaces. The main characteristic of an interactive tabletop is a large horizontal screen which is used as display and interactive surface at the same time (Bellucci et al., 2014). It has been thoroughly stated in prior research that interactive tabletops have a positive impact on collaboration (e.g. Scott et al, 2003) and collaborative learning (Rick et al., 2011).

Hornecker et al. (2008) explored awareness in co-located settings through negative and positive awareness indicators. Negative awareness indicators are i) *interference* (e.g., reaching for same object) and ii) *verbal monitoring* ("what did you do there?"), while positive awareness indicators are i) *reaction without explicit*

request, ii) *parallel work on same activity without verbal coordination*, among others. In this paper, we will explore *"pointing gestures towards other users' personal areas"* as an additional awareness mechanism.
Falcão & Price (2009) run a user study that explored collaborative activity on a tangible tabletop to support co-located learning about the physics of light. They found that the 'interference' activity happened both accidentally and intentionally when children purposely changed arrangements to give demonstrations or help each other out by giving instructions, both physically and verbally. This led the children group through a productive process of collective exploration and knowledge construction.
Our research is also related to information visualisation, shared control, territoriality, and multi-view tabletops. Stewart et al. (1999) has shown that shared control resulted in less collaboration due to parallel working without having to share the input device. Lissermann et al. (2014) introduced *Permulin*, a mixed-focus collaboration on multi-view tabletops, which provides distinct private views or a group view that is overlaid with private contents, thus allowing easy and seamless transitions along the entire spectrum between tightly and loosely coupled collaboration. Most recently, Woodward et al. (2018) adapted the social regulation and group processes of Rogat & Linnenbrink-Garcia (2001) and broke down the social interactions into 4 main themes: *Social Regulation*, *Positive Socioemotional Interactions* (encouraging participation), *Negative Socioemotional Interactions* (discouraging participation), and *Interactions*. Under *Interactions*, they included *Roles*, which is about "respecting or not respecting assigned role, enforcing roles, pointing to other area". This paper lies upon this kind of *interaction* and *roles*.
Since we are exploring pointing gestures in multi-user collaborative environments, cooperative gestures, as described in Morris et al. (2006) are of interest in our research. They introduced the so-called *symmetry* axis referring to whether participants perform identical or distinct actions, and *parallelism* as the relative timing of each contributor's axis. An *additive* gesture is one which is meaningful when performed by a single user, but whose meaning is amplified when simultaneously performed by all members of the group.

3. Research goal

At Luxembourg Institute of Science and Technology, there have been several user studies on tabletop interfaces conducted (e.g., Ras et al., 2013; Lahure et al., 2018; Anastasiou et al., 2018), mostly within the context of collaborative problem-solving. Within the past project GETUI[1], Anastasiou et al. (2018) examined the relevance of gestures in the assessment of group collaborative skills. The current project ORBIT[2] has the goal of enhancing users' awareness of their collaboration strategies by providing them with tasks and tools that induce their collaboration and create overall a positive user experience. To do so, a problem-solving activity is designed and implemented through an iterative design process, in which tasks and features are designed that repeatedly put users in a situation to collaborate (see Sunnen et al., 2019). ORBIT benefits from the potentials of both tangible and multi-touch interaction in terms of promoting collaboration.
As far as awareness is concerned, according to Endsley (1995), situation awareness refers to "knowing what is going on" and involves states of knowledge as well as dynamic processes of perception and action.
In this paper, we explore the situations of low awareness and define them as "situations where explicit awareness work occurs", according to Hornecker et al. (2008). Table 1 lists a few of such low awareness situations that happened in our user study. As a reaction to obtain and maintain awareness in these situations, a person might employ exaggerated manual actions to draw attention (Hornecker et al., 2008).

Examples of low awareness situations
New information is revealed (e.g. new features or hidden items) and users are not yet familiar with them.
A suggestion for a route is made, but one or more users are hesitant, thus inactive (no speaking & not pressing any buttons).
One or more users take a bad decision by moving the rover towards an unfavorable cell.
Two or more users disagree verbally.

Table 1: Examples of low awareness situations

It is worth mentioning that this list is non-exhaustive and these situations are mostly context-dependent.
In this paper, we will focus only on the pointing gestures as a reaction to low awareness situations, and by this, we mean pointing gestures addressed to the area of the tabletop where another participant is responsible for. Table 2 presents such cases along with some relevant figures underneath (Fig. 1, 2, 3). After we describe our user study within the ORBIT project (Section 4), we count those pointing gesture occurrences in our data analysis (Section 5).

Pointing gestures as awareness work
One user pointing to another user's area (Fig. 1)
Two users pointing to another (same) user's area (Fig. 2)
User A points to users B's area and user C points to user A's area (Fig. 3)
One user pointing to and touching at another user's area

Table 2: Pointing gestures as awareness work

Figure 1: One user pointing to another user's personal area

[1] https://www.list.lu/en/research/project/getui/, 17.02.2020

[2] https://www.orbit.team/, 17.02.2020

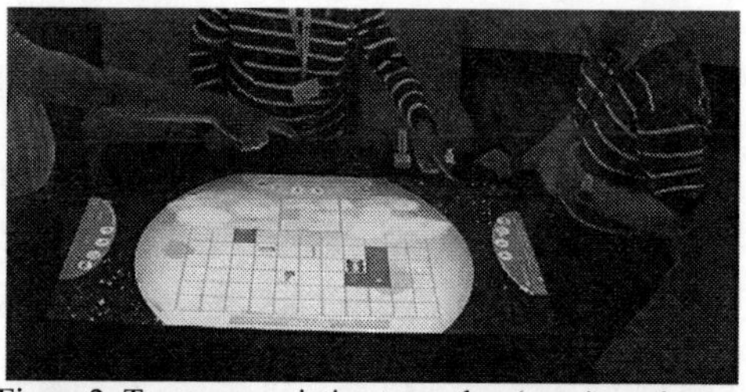

Figure 2: Two users pointing to another (same) user's area

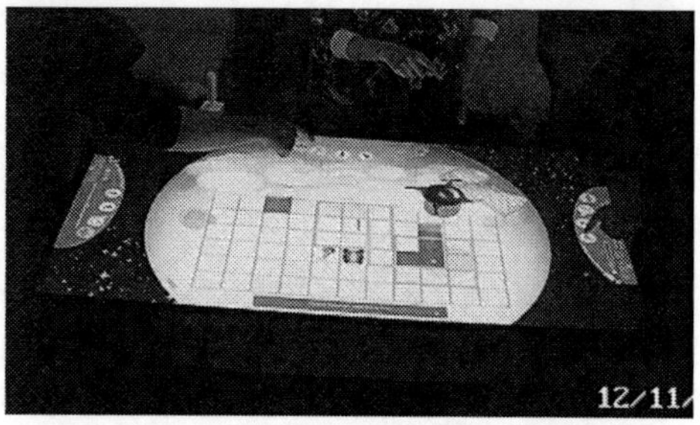

Figure 3: Users pointing at different directions

4. User Study

In this Section we describe our user study design (4.1), as well as the task of the participants, i.e. the computer-simulated problem (4.2).

4.1 Study design

The user study was an experimental between-subjects design with 5 groups consisting of 3 participants each. Depending on the analysis objective, the analysis unit might be the group (n=5) or the individual (n=15). The participants were not informed by any means about the task that they had to solve which is in line with the concept of a *microworld.* Microworlds are defined by Edwards (1991) as the instantiation of an artificial environment that behaves according to a custom set of mathematical rules or scientific subdomains. Moreover, the participants did not know each other, as this familiarity would have biased the interference. The occupational background of the participants is heterogeneous: 6 were employees of municipal departments, 6 elementary school teachers, 2 computer science researchers and 1 civil engineering researcher. They have never used a tangible tabletop before. The groups were gender and age-mixed: 10 male and 5 female; 5 were aged between 25-34, 5 between 35-44, and 5 between 45-54. Groups spoke in different languages; 3 groups spoke in Luxembourgish, 1 in French, and 1 in English. The potential differences in gesture performance due to the language spoken is out of the scope of this paper.

As far as the technological setup is concerned, there was the multitouch table *Multitaction*, which that recognizes fingertips, fingers, hands and objects simultaneously (see Fig.1-3). There were four fixed cameras placed at the top, front, left and right angle. For our gesture analysis & annotation, we used the front camera view.

4.2 Computer-simulated problem

The computer-simulated problem in this user study visualised at the tabletop is a joint problem-solving activity developed in the context of the ORBIT project and is called *Orbitia. Orbitia* aims to support participants in developing their collaboration methods. In the activity narrative, provided as a textual instruction on the tabletop before the commencement of the experiment[3], participants are located on *Orbitia*, an imaginary planet where they need to act as space mining crew in order to mine valuable minerals and ship them to earth. The main task of participants is to steer a rover and operate a radar drone on the planet surface to find and collect required minerals. In parallel, participants need to deal with limitations of the environment, such as obstacles, energy and movement constraints.

The activity has three missions and takes place within a 9 × 11 grid presented at the centre of the tabletop screen.

Additional to the rover, there are other icons:

1) *Minerals*: the main collectable items; participants are informed about the number of required minerals at the beginning of each mission as task description.
2) *Sharp rocks*: steering the rover to the cells containing sharp rocks causes damage to the rover and makes the rover unable to move, unless a repair is done by participants. Damaging the rover more than three times causes failing the mission.
3) *Batteries*: each movement of the rover costs one unit of energy and participants need to recharge the rover when needed by stepping on a cell containing a battery.
4) *Canyons* are cells marked darker than normal grid cells; leading the rover to a canyon results in destroying the rover and failing the mission.
5) *Dust storm area*: furthermore, a part of the grid is marked as cloudy-like area. According to the activity scenario, this area is affected by a dust storm and therefore, the items located in any of those cells are hidden. Participants need to use the radar drone in order to find and reveal the hidden items.

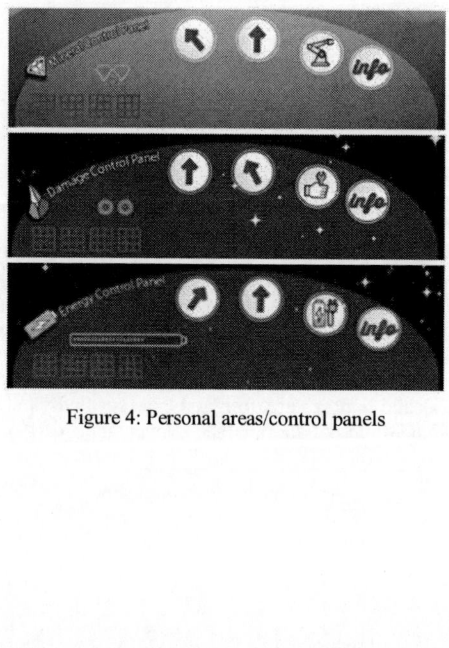

Figure 4: Personal areas/control panels

[3] This narrative was the only instruction given to the participants.

It is important to note that there were three personal areas known as control panels in three sides of the screen (see Fig. 4); The idea is to give each user a specific personal area in front of his/her position, providing them with the opportunity of individual control over certain aspects of the activity: *mining*, *energy* and *damage*. No information was given to the users prior to the study regarding the control panels and the users' specific responsibility. Nevertheless, the distributed location and design of the control panels, led the users to place themselves in front of each panel and find out about their own specific responsibility.

5. Multimodal corpus

As a result from our observational user study, we collected in total *168.68 minutes* of audiovisual material. This audiovisual corpus can be used for many purposes, such as conversational analysis, gesture analysis, complex problem-solving assessment, and many others. In the next Section, we present the results of the complex problem-solving assessment, and the pointing gesture occurrences in low awareness situations.

5.1 Data analysis

Here we present the quantitative data analysis results of the complex problem-solving assessment (5.1.1), which is categorized into two measurements: i) response time and ii) errors. Moreover, we measured the pointing gesture occurrences towards other users' personal areas (5.1.2), as presented in Table 2.

5.1.1 Response time & errors in problem-solving

We looked at the total response time of each group, i.e. the time each group needed to solve the collaborative problem in total (see Table 3) as well as the errors the groups made in total. In *Orbitia*, we have defined an error as destroying the rover, which could have happened if the users had run three times over a cell containing sharp rocks or led the rover in a canyon cell, or run out of energy.

Group Nr.	Response time	Errors
Group 1	49:21	0
Group 2	24:32	8
Group 3	42:05	5
Group 4	23:02	0
Group 5	30:08	1

Table 3: Groups' response times and error rates

Group 4 was the fastest group with 23:02 min, while the slowest group was Group 1 with 49:25 min. The slowest group spent a lot of time analysing and discussing before they manipulate the tangible objects and items of the activity. This had as an impact on the complete lack of errors (n=0). Interesting is, though, that while Group 2 and Group 4 solved the problem almost at the same time with a slight difference of 1:30 min, Group 2 made 8 errors, while Group 4 made 0 errors. This shows that making errors results in more trials, but does not necessarily decelerate the process of collaborative problem-solving.

5.1.2 Gesture occurrences

After annotating the videos with ELAN (Wittenburg et al. 2006), we found that there are in total 341 such pointing gestures directed to the personal area of the peers. Table 4 depicts the gesture occurrences performed by each participant and in each group.

Users	Group 1	Group 2	Group 3	Group 4	Group 5
A	56	10	68	10	8
B	18	11	19	15	24
C	30	4	15	32	31
Total	**104**	**25**	**102**	**57**	**53**

Table 4: Pointing gestures towards other users' personal areas performed by each user in each group

Based on the relative gesture numbers (gesture per second), group 4 performed most gestures. Thus, we deduce that the more frequent the pointing gestures produced by the groups, the less number of errors made. It should be noted that there are some extreme cases, such as user A in Group 3, who performed many more gestures than all other users. In this case, we speak about a person who wants to take the lead in the problem-solving activity.

Table 5 presents descriptive statistics about the kind of gesture occurrences during low awareness situations.

Gestures occurrences during low awareness situations	*#gestures*
One user pointing to another participant's area (Fig. 1)	312
Two users pointing to another (same) user's area (Fig. 2)	4
User A pointing to user B's area and user C pointing to user A's area (Fig. 3)	2
One user pointing to and touching at another user's area	11

Table 5: Gesture occurrences towards other users' personal areas in our scenario (*Orbitia*)

The results show that the biggest amount of gestures are when one user points to another user's area (95%). That two users point simultaneously or consecutively to another user's area is quite uncommon, since users retracted their gestures when they saw that their peer is going to perform the same gesture as they planned, so they considered it as a non-*additive* gesture (according to Morris et al., 2006). The most seldom cases were the ones that two users pointed at different personal areas. There were also a few cases, where one user not only pointed to the other user's area, but also touched it. These situations are indeed rare, however, the user who manipulates someone else's area, is considering him/herself as a lead person, while in the other cases (pointing only, without touching), it is clear that the users are trying to help and not taking the lead action.

5.1.2.1 A gesture taxonomy

A taxonomy of gestures being performed on tangible tabletops, taking into account both the 2D and 3D space was developed earlier (Anastasiou & Bergmann, 2016; Anastasiou et al., 2018). We followed the taxonomy of McNeill (1992), and focused particularly on *gesticulation* (further classified into *iconic*, *metaphoric*, *rhythmic*, *cohesive*, and *deictic* gestures), but also *emblems* and *adaptors*. As for gesture taxonomy from an HCI perspective, we followed Quek (1995) who classified meaningful gestures into *communicative* and *manipulative* gestures. *Manipulative* gestures can occur either on the desktop in a 2-D interaction using a direct manipulation device, as a 3-D interaction involving empty-handed movements to mimic manipulations of physical objects, or by manipulating actual physical objects that map onto a virtual object in TUIs. We focus particularly on the first and third categorization of manipulative gestures. Therefore, in our taxonomy we have *manipulative* gestures, which are restricted to screen-based activity (Table 5) and *communicative co-speech* gestures, which happen in the 3D space, such as *pointing* & *iconic*, but also affect displays, *adaptors* and *emblems*. In our setting, many pointing gestures were *beats* (McNeil, 1992) or *batonic* gestures, which are simple, brief, repetitive, and coordinated with the speech prosody used either to emphasize information on the other users' personal area or to gain the interlocutor overall attention. Van den Hoven & Mazalek (2010) defined *tangible gesture interaction* as the use of physical devices for facilitating, supporting, enhancing, or tracking gestures people make for digital interaction purposes. As in the case of Price et al. (2010), in our study we had also a mixture of manipulative and communicative gestural interaction.

Manipulative	placing removing tracing rotating resizing tapping sweeping flicking holding

Table 5: Touch-based or manipulative gestures

The taxonomy of pointing gestures is now extended after our user study. Now the categories pointing gesture to a *personal area of other participant* and *pointing and touching personal area of other participant* are added.

Pointing	object(s)
	tabletop (shared space)
	personal area of other participant
	other participant(s)
	self-pointing
	pointing and touching personal area of other participant
Iconic	encircling with whole hand
	encircling with index finger
	moving an open hand forward/backward
	moving an open hand downwards vertically
Adaptors	head scratching
	mouth scratching
	nail biting
	hair twirling
Emblems	thumps up
	victory sign
	fist(s) pump

Table 6: Mid-air gestures with new annotation categories under pointing (in italics)

6. Discussion and Future Work

In this paper, we described a user study on collaborative problem-solving using an interactive tabletop. We examined only the explicit awareness work in the form of pointing to the other participant's personal area. The average number of such pointing gestures per minute in total was 1.96. From the annotations, we can deduce that these gestures mostly happen in the familiarization phase, i.e. the first minutes of the experiment, where the participants familiarize themselves with the features and information of the problem-solving scenario.

Certainly, the way the problem-solving scenario is designed is responsible for the frequency of such gesture occurrences. The technological setup, the task of the participants, the territoriality as well as the shape/size of tangibles have a great influence on the resulting interaction patterns. It is common fact in the literature that gestures aid both communicators and recipients in problem-solving (Lozano & Tversky, 2006) and facilitate thinking and speaking. Real decision-making and problem-solving can become highly complex and require the expertise of a heterogeneous group of communicators. In these situations, it is essential that users quickly obtain and maintain awareness of the situation and others. Therefore, it is important to know how to evaluate and assess such pointing gestures as reaction to low awareness. Indeed, it is difficult to observe "pure" low awareness situations and thus isolate corresponding gestures. In our microworld scenario, we defined personal areas/control stations for each participant, so when a pointing gesture was addressed to this area of another user, it was counted as a gesture occurrence during low awareness situation. From our gesture analysis, we can deduce that those gestures happen when one user is not reacting fast enough, performing adaptors (head or mouth scratching) or taking a bad decision by moving the rover to an unfavorable cell. In parallel, the speech is often accompanied with loud voice and the utterances are targeted personally.

As far as future work is concerned, we plan to run more user studies with *Orbitia* with more groups speaking the same mother language. With regards to the annotations, it is important to annotate how the person who was pointed to, reacted: verbally, physically, or no reaction. If verbally, what did (s)he say (conversational analysis) and if physically, which kind of gestures (s)he performed. Some of the arguments were at negotiational phase "*We do not need to hurry, it is the number of moves*", whereas some others were targeted personally to the other participants: "*You have not used this wisely*", "*You have to think before we move*". We also plan to annotate the utterances according to the social regulation patterns of Woodward et al. (2018). Awareness work mechanisms will be enhanced by annotating the change of body position as well as facial expressions and eye gaze. We will also look at using automated systems for gesture annotation to speed up the time-consuming task of annotation. In this case, the automatically recognized manipulative gestures can be also automatically annotated in the system.

Not rare is the case that the instructions of other participants is not semantically correct. This means, that the people that interfere believe that momentarily they give the correct instruction, but often, they self-reflect again (often during their instruction) and correct themselves either verbally (through repair) or physically (retracting gestures) or both. Therefore, the annotation should also include the semantic connotation of the interference: right/wrong. The same holds for the reaction of the pointed person, as it is often the case that (s)he just listens to and obeys the instructions of the peers without self-reflecting if these are right or wrong.

Last but not least, in this paper, we have presented only descriptive statistics; after collecting more data, we will run inferential statistics to confirm the statistical significance between gesture occurrences, error rates, and response times.

7. Acknowledgements

We would like to thank the Luxembourg National Research Fund (FNR) for funding this research under the CORE scheme (Ref. 11632733).

8. References

8.1 Bibliographical References

Anastasiou, D. & Bergmann, K. (2016). A Gesture-Speech Corpus on a Tangible Interface. *Proceedings of Multimodal Corpora Workshop*, LREC Conference.

Anastasiou, D., Ras, E., Fal., M., (2018), Assessment of Collaboration and Feedback on Gesture Performance, in: *Proceedings of the Technology-enhanced Assessment (TEA) conference* 2018, Springer, 219-232.

Bellucci, A., Malizia, A., & Aedo, I. (2014). Light on horizontal interactive surfaces: Input space for tabletop computing. *ACM Computing Surveys (CSUR)*, *46*(3), 1-42.

Edwards, L.D. (1991). The design and analysis of a mathematical microworld. *Journal of Educational Computing Research*, 12(1), 77-94.

Endsley, M. R. (1995). Toward a Theory of Situation Awareness in Dynamic Systems. *Human Factors*, *37*(1), 32-64.

Falcão, T. P., & Price, S. (2009). What have you done! the role of 'interference' in tangible environments for supporting collaborative learning. In *CSCL* (1), 325-334.

Griffin, P., Care, E., & McGaw, B. (2012). The changing role of education and schools. In P. Griffin, B. McGaw, & E. Care (Eds.), *Assessment and Teaching 21st Century Skills*, Heidelberg: Springer, 1-15.

Gutwin, C., & Greenberg, S. (2002). A descriptive framework of workspace awareness for real-time groupware. *Computer Supported Cooperative Work* (CSCW), 11(3-4), 411-446.

Hornecker, E., Marshall, P., Dalton, S., & Rogers, Y. (2008). Collaboration and Interference: Awareness with Mice or Touch Input. *Proceedings of Computer Supported Cooperative Work* (CSCW'08), San Diego, USA. ACM Press.

Lahure, C., & Maquil, V. (2018). Slowing Down Interactions on Tangible Tabletop Interfaces. *i-com*, *17*(3), 189-199.

Lissermann, R., Huber, J., Schmitz, M., Steimle, J., & Mühlhäuser, M. (2014). Permulin: mixed-focus collaboration on multi-view tabletops. *Proceedings of the SIGCHI Conference on Human Factors in Computing Systems,* 3191-3200.

Lozano, S. C., & Tversky, B. (2006). RETRACTED: Communicative gestures facilitate problem solving for both communicators and recipients.

McNeill, D. (1992). *Hand and mind: What gestures reveal about thought*, Chicago: University of Chicago Press.

Morris, M.R, et al. (2006). Cooperative gestures: multi-user gestural interactions for co-located groupware. *Proceedings of CHI 2006*, 1201-1210,

Organisation for Economic Co-operation and Development (OECD). 2013. *PISA 2015 draft collaborative problem solving framework*, https://www.oecd.org/pisa/pisaproducts/Draft%20PISA%202015%20Collaborative%20Problem%20Solving%20Framework%20.pdf.

Price, S., Sheridan, J.G., & Pontual Falcao, T. (2010). Action and representa-tion in tangible systems: implications for design of learning interactions. *Proc. 4th Int. Conf. Tangible, Embedded, and Embodied Interaction* (TEI '10), 145-152.

Quek, F.K.H. (1995). Eyes in the interface. *Image and Vision Computing*, 13(6), 511-525.

Ras, E. et al. (2013). Empirical studies on a tangible user interface for technology-based assessment: Insights and emerging challenges. *International Journal of e-Assessment*, 3(1), 201-241.

Rick, J., Marshall, P., & Yuill, N. (2011). Beyond one-size-fits-all: How interactive tabletops support collaborative learning. *Proceedings of the 10th International Conference on Interaction Design and Children*, 109-117.

Rogat, T.K., & Linnenbrink-Garcia, L. (2011). Socially Shared Regulation in Collaborative Groups: An Analysis of the Interplay Between Quality of Social Regulation and Group Processes. *Cognition and Instruction* 29, 4 (2011), 375-415.

Scott, S. D., Grant, K. D., & Mandryk, R. L. (2003). System guidelines for co-located, collaborative work on a tabletop display. In *ECSCW 2003,* Springer, Dordrecht, 159-178.

Stewart, J., Bederson, B. B., & Druin, A. (1999). Single Display Groupware: A Model for Co-present Collaboration. *Proceedings of SIGCHI Conference of Human Factors in Computing Systems* (CHI 99), 286 – 293, Pittsburgh, USA. ACM Press.

Sunnen, P., Arend, B., Heuser, S., Afkari, H., & Maquil, V. (2019). Designing collaborative scenarios on tangible tabletop interfaces-insights from the implementation of paper prototypes in the context of a multidisciplinary design workshop. *Proceedings of 17th European Conference on Computer-Supported Cooperative Work.* European Society for Socially Embedded Technologies.

Wittenburg P et al. (2006). ELAN: a professional framework for multimodality research. *Proceedings of the 5th Conference on Language Resources and Evaluation*, 1556-1559.

Woodward, J., Esmaeili, S., Jain, A., Bell, J., Ruiz, J., & Anthony, L. (2018). Investigating Separation of Territories and Activity Roles in Children's Collaboration around Tabletops. *Proceedings of the ACM on Human-Computer Interaction*, 2(CSCW), 1-21.

Proceedings of ONION 2020: Workshop on peOple in laNguage, vIsiOn and the miNd, pages 28–33
Language Resources and Evaluation Conference (LREC 2020), Marseille, 11–16 May 2020

Improving Sentiment Analysis with Biofeedback Data

Daniel Schlör*, Albin Zehe*, Konstantin Kobs*, Blerta Veseli, Franziska Westermeier, Larissa Brübach, Daniel Roth, Marc Erich Latoschik, Andreas Hotho
Julius-Maximilians University Würzburg
Am Hubland, 97074 Würzburg, Germany
{schloer, zehe, kobs, veseli, hotho}@informatik.uni-wuerzburg.de
{franziska.westermeier, larissa.bruebach}@stud-mail.uni-wuerzburg.de
{daniel.roth, marc.latoschik}@uni-wuerzburg.de

Abstract

Humans frequently are able to read and interpret emotions of others by directly taking verbal and non-verbal signals in human-to-human communication into account or to infer or even experience emotions from mediated stories. For computers, however, emotion recognition is a complex problem: Thoughts and feelings are the roots of many behavioural responses and they are deeply entangled with neurophysiological changes within humans. As such, emotions are very subjective, often are expressed in a subtle manner, and are highly depending on context. For example, machine learning approaches for text-based sentiment analysis often rely on incorporating sentiment lexicons or language models to capture the contextual meaning. This paper explores if and how we further can enhance sentiment analysis using biofeedback of humans which are experiencing emotions while reading texts. Specifically, we record the heart rate and brain waves of readers that are presented with short texts which have been annotated with the emotions they induce. We use these physiological signals to improve the performance of a lexicon-based sentiment classifier. We find that the combination of several biosignals can improve the ability of a text-based classifier to detect the presence of a sentiment in a text on a per-sentence level.

Keywords: sentiment detection, brain-computer-interface, bio-sensing, affective computing

1. Introduction

Sentiment analysis has long been an active field of research in the natural language processing (NLP) community due to its widespread applicability and its potential to guide people in important decisions (Wang et al., 2012; Rill et al., 2014; Kobs et al., 2020). However, sentiment analysis for texts except tweets and product reviews, especially in languages other than English, has proven to be a challenging task, mostly due to the difficulty of getting sufficient training data (Zehe et al., 2017; Gangula and Mamidi, 2018; Schmidt and Burghardt, 2018).

According to Caicedo and Van Beuzekom (2006), emotional response typically has three components: subjective feeling (e.g., self-report), motor expression (e.g., facial expression), and physiological arousal (e.g., heart rate and brain waves). A labelling process typical for sentiment analysis is based purely on self-reports. Such reports are very time-consuming and tedious tasks, and they are highly prone to the individual's subjective rating.

In contrast, emotion recognition, or emotion identification based on objective measurements of neurophysiological signals is common in the field of affective computing, meaning "computing that relates to, arises from, or influences emotion" (Picard, 2000, p. 1). In studies about measuring emotions using neurophysiological data, emotions are often triggered by perceptual stimuli, e.g. visual (Bhardwaj et al., 2015), auditory (Lin et al., 2010) or audiovisual stimuli (Kimmatkar and Babu, 2018). However, there still is no clear consensus about the appropriate approach to model and hence to classify emotions, i.e., if emotions are discrete constructs or if they are on continuous scales separated in groups. Various approaches exist, for example, to classify emotions in terms of valence (neutral, positive, negative), in terms of the quadrants of the valence-arousal model (Lin et al., 2010), or even in terms of different levels of extent of valence and arousal (Horlings et al., 2008).

So far, measurements of neurophysiological signals are not common in NLP research. In this paper, we propose to merge both approaches, sentiment analysis of annotated texts and objective measurements of neurophysiological signals. Our approach uses affordable and convenient devices, i.e., a smart watch and a consumer-grade electroencephalography (EEG) headband. To this end, we

i) make a dataset available that includes sentiment annotations, as well as two types of biofeedback data, namely heart rate and EEG data[1],

ii) perform an initial study showing that the biofeedback contains signals useful for sentiment analysis, and

iii) discuss possible extensions and directions for future work, where we believe that incorporating information from biofeedback into sentiment classifiers will be helpful.

In our initial study using German texts, we find that either heart rate or EEG data can not be used by itself to predict sentiment as accurately as a text sentiment classifier. However, by combining a simple text sentiment classifier with heart rate and EEG data, we can improve the detection of presence or absence of sentiment in the text.

In the following Section 2 we provide an overview of related work. In Section 3 our task and approach are then described. After giving details for our dataset in Section 4, in Sections 5 and 6 we describe and discuss our results. We conclude the paper in Section 7 with a summary of our findings and an outlook on future work.

* equal contribution

[1] `https://professor-x.de/datasets/dataset_onion_biofeedback.zip`

2. Related Work

There is a large body of work on detecting sentiment from text. A full overview is out of scope for this paper, so we refer to the recent survey in (Zhang et al., 2018). Most recent sentiment analysis methods are based on pre-trained transformer architectures such as BERT (Devlin et al., 2018; Munikar et al., 2019). However, these models still require a rather large amount of data to fine-tune, which is not available for every language and domain.

Similarly, there exists some work investigating the detection of emotions from biofeedback data. The study by Choi et al. (2017) indicates that it is possible to detect unhappy emotions that were induced by visual stimuli from heart rate variability.

In an EEG setting, visual stimuli achieved high accuracy in emotion classification (Petrantonakis and Hadjileontiadis, 2009). For other stimuli such as audio, a link from the recorded EEG data to the perceived emotion was also reported (Lin et al., 2010). Further, affect detection using an EEG was proposed to visualize emotional states of users augmenting avatar-mediated communications (Roth et al., 2019c; Roth et al., 2019b).

Using EEG data for sentiment analysis was previously proposed in (Gu et al., 2014). In their work, subjects were instructed to visualize single words in their thoughts. Their EEG response was then used as input to machine learning models to predict the valence of these words. One subject achieved better scores for concrete words, while abstract words were better estimated by lexicons.

Multimodal emotion recognition using EEG, pulse, and skin conductance with audio-visual stimuli was also performed (Takahashi, 2004).

To the best of our knowledge, our study is the first to combine lexical sentiment analysis approaches with heart rate and EEG signals collected in a natural text reading task.

3. Methodology

We define two separate sentence-level tasks for our study: *sentiment detection* and *sentiment classification*. The first task aims to determine whether or not a sentence conveys any emotion (regardless of its polarity), while the second provides a more fine-grained classification of sentences into the three classes *negative*, *neutral*, and *positive*. We hypothesize that biofeedback is a good indicator for at least the first task, as physiological activity can change when feeling both positive and negative emotions.

For both of these tasks, we evaluate classifiers based on a) the text of the sentence, b) the readers' biofeedback data collected while reading the sentence, and c) a combination of both.

3.1. Text Based Sentiment Classifiers

Due to the small amount of available data, we use the lexicon based classifier provided by the German version of TextBlob[2], which assigns each word a sentiment score from the range $[-1, 1]$ and then calculates the overall sentiment score for a sentence. It also features a negation detection that multiplies sentiments of negated words by -0.5. Using the resulting polarity score $v(s)$ for one sentence s, we can define thresholds for the classification of a sentence into one of the desired classes. We classify a sentence as *positive* if $v(s) > 0.25$, *negative* if $v(s) < -0.25$, and *neutral* otherwise. In the sentiment detection setting, we classify a sentence to contain sentiment if and only if $|v(s)| > 0.25$.

[2] https://pypi.python.org/pypi/textblob-de/.

3.2. Biofeedback Based Sentiment Classifiers

In this study, we compare Random Forests (RF) and linear Support Vector Machines (SVMs) for the detection and classification of sentiment from biofeedback. For both machine learning models, we use the implementation in scikit-learn (Pedregosa et al., 2011) with default parameters. We modify the number of decision trees in the Random Forest to be ten due to the faster training time and better generalization for this low data setting.

Both classifiers receive input based on the readers' biofeedback while reading the sentence that is to be classified. Let $B_u^c(t)$ be the value of channel $c \in C = \{$ heart rate, EEG_1, ..., $\text{EEG}_n\}$ for the biofeedback data from user u at timestamp t. For each sentence s, $\text{begin}_u(s)$ and $\text{end}_u(s)$ give the timestamp when reader u starts and finishes reading the sentence, respectively. All timestamps recorded for user u and channel c are given in T_u^c. Then, $T_u^c(s) = [t_b, \ldots, t_e]$ with $\text{begin}_u(s) \leq t_i < \text{end}_u(s)$ describes all timestamps for user u and channel c which were recorded while reading the sentence s. The sample-rate sr_c describes how many timestamps and thus sensor values are recorded per second. From these time series, we derive the features for our classifiers.

3.2.1. Heart Rate Features

For the heart rate data, we define $ba_u^{hr}(s)$ as the absolute average heart rate of user u while reading sentence s:

$$ba_u^{hr}(s) = \frac{\sum\limits_{t \in T_u^{hr}(s)} B_u^{hr}(t)}{|T_u^{hr}(s)|} . \quad (1)$$

The relative average heart rate of user u is normalized per user, given as

$$b_u^{hr}(s) = \frac{ba_u^{hr}(s) - min(B_u^{hr})}{max(B_u^{hr}) - min(B_u^{hr})} . \quad (2)$$

We represent a sentence s using the values $b_u^{hr}(s)$ for all users as well as their deltas, that is

$$\hat{b}_u^{hr}(s) = b_u^{hr}(s) - b_u^{hr}(s-1) . \quad (3)$$

3.2.2. EEG Features

For the EEG data, we use Fourier transformed and filtered values to better represent the common spectral bands present in brain activity (Murugappan and Murugappan, 2013). We select the time window where the reader u reads the sentence s, and select all sensor values with timestamps within this window.

$$\begin{aligned} b_u^{eeg_i}(s) &= [B_u^{eeg_i}(t_b), ..., B_u^{eeg_i}(t_e)] \\ &\text{with } [t_b, ..., t_e] = T_u^{eeg_i}(s) \end{aligned} \quad (4)$$

For each EEG channel $i \in \{1, \ldots, 8\}$ and sentence s Fourier transformation is applied to this window, producing $\hat{b}_u^{eeg_i}(s)$.
We use $\hat{b}_u^{eeg_i}(s)$ for all EEG channels and all users to represent sentence s. Note, that $\hat{b}_u^{eeg_i}(s)$ contains all frequencies between 0 and $\frac{sr_{eeg}}{2}$ in a fine-grained resolution. We reduce the number of features by a) applying a band-pass filter between 13 and 30 Hz to remove unwanted frequencies and b) applying a pincipal component analysis (PCA). We found 3 principal components to work best.

4. Dataset

This section describes the dataset of texts annotated with heart rates, which we enrich with sentiment annotations as well as EEG data for one additional reader.
For our study, we use the BioReaderData dataset presented by Schlör et al. (2019) consisting of 4 medium-length texts in German language with different topics that should trigger different emotional reactions. The texts contained in the dataset have a length between 502 and 633 words and are described in the following:

a) *Kangaroo*[3]: an excerpt from a humorous narrative book,

b) *Dogs*[4]: a neutrally written factual text from National Geographic,

c) *Genie*[5]: a short report about the tragic story of a feral child with many negatively connoted words, and

d) *James*[6]: a neutrally written chronological description of a child's murder.

The existing dataset contains heart rate measurements of 15 German native speakers that were reading the given texts using the BioReader app. Subjects were equipped with a Polar M600 smartwatch that measures heart rate with a sampling frequency $sr_{hr} = 2$Hz. The app captures the reading progress, such that heart rate data can be aligned to the text.

Extending the Dataset with Sentiment Information In order to perform sentiment analysis on the dataset, we let three subjects annotate each sentence in the dataset on a three-part polarity scale as either *negative*, *neutral*, or *positive*. A majority voting then determined the gold standard label, discarding all sentences where a majority vote was not possible. This resulted in a dataset with 164 sentences. A description of the texts in terms of sentence counts as well as label distribution is shown in Table 1.

[3]Marc-Uwe Kling, Die Känguru-Chroniken: Ansichten eines vorlauten Beuteltiers "Theorie und Praxis", Ullstein eBooks, 2010

[4]https://www.nationalgeographic.de/wissenschaft/2018/07/wohin-verschwanden-die-ersten-hunde-amerikas

[5]https://www1.wdr.de/stichtag/stichtag-554.html

[6]https://de.wikipedia.org/wiki/Mord_an_James_Bulger&stableid=176294324

Text	# Sentences	# Neg.	# Neu.	# Pos.
Kangaroo	56 (50)	20	21	9
Dogs	31 (31)	5	17	9
Genie	45 (43)	29	12	2
James	42 (40)	28	8	4
Total	174 (164)	82	58	24

Table 1: The number of sentences per text in the dataset as well as the number of sentences that are labeled as negative, neutral, and positive by a majority vote of three annotators. The number of sentences per text that received a label in the majority vote is given in parentheses.

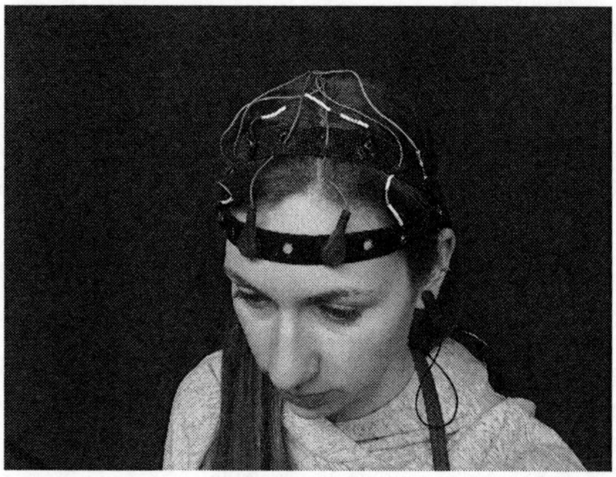

Figure 1: OpenBCI headband as worn for EEG data collection during our study.

Extending the Dataset with EEG Data To extend the dataset with EEG measurements, we used a headband with an OpenBCI[7] Cyton board (PIC32MX250F128B microcontroller) and 8 electrodes. Electrode placements were made near the frontal and the parietal lobes at the positions Fp1, Fp2, F7, F8, T3, T4, F3 and F4 according to the 10-20 system, as these were shown to yield good features to capture the emotional state (Lin et al., 2010; Bos and others, 2006). Previous work has shown that emotion classification can be achieved with a limited number of electrodes (Bhardwaj et al., 2015). The setup is depicted in Figure 1.
We presented the sentences from BioReaderData dataset to the reader while capturing their EEG data. The EEG data was obtained with a sampling rate of $f_{eeg} = 250$ Hz, resulting in 378704 data points.
After obtaining the EEG data, the reader was asked to review the annotated gold standard sentiment labels with respect to the perceived sentiment. The reader agreed with the gold standard label for 95% of the samples. All 8 cases of disagreement involved a sentiment change from or to neutral, indicating that these sentences can be considered borderline cases where the presence of sentiment is arguable. We use the EEG data for all sentences as biofeedback, including the sentences with disagreement since this setup is the more difficult task and also more realistic, since for

[7]https://openbci.com

Classifier	Detection (RF/SVM)	Classification (RF/SVM)
Majority Vote	39.3	22.2
Stratified Random	51.2	31.0
Text	55.1	**46.4**
Heart Rate	55.0/43.3	33.8/26.2
EEG	46.5/49.2	31.1/31.7
Text, Heart Rate	55.7/43.5	39.9/27.9
Text, EEG	51.2/48.6	36.1/34.0
Heart Rate, EEG	52.9/49.4	37.7/31.7
Text, Heart Rate, EEG	**58.5**/51.3	38.5/35.4

Table 2: Results for sentiment detection and classification. All numbers in percent macro-averaged F1-scores. Where applicable, the first number is the performance of a Random Forest, the second number the performance of a linear SVM. The best performance for each task is given in bold, the better model for each feature set is underlined.

larger scale study the assessment of individual sentiment perception per sample will not be feasible.

5. Experiments

We perform experiments on the BioReaderData dataset with both classifiers, Random Forest and linear SVM, for the tasks of sentiment detection and sentiment classification. We evaluate all feature set combinations to better understand the influence a certain feature set has on the overall performance. Additionally, we employ two baselines: i) Majority vote, that always predicts the most frequent class: *non-neutral / emotional* in sentiment detection and *negative* in sentiment classification. ii) Stratified random, that takes the class distribution of the training set into account and samples the prediction from this distribution. All baselines and classifiers are evaluated using a stratified 5-fold cross-validation that is repeated 10 times. We report macro-averaged F1-scores for all methods.

5.1. Sentiment Detection

For the sentiment detection, we merge the positive and negative labels in the BioReaderData data. Applying all classifiers to the data results in the macro F1-scores reported in the second column of Table 2. Training a Random Forest on heart rate data of 15 subjects results in a comparable sentiment detection performance as the text based method. While text and heart rate achieve better performance than the baseline methods, using EEG data alone did not perform better than random sampling from the training data's class distribution. Combining all three feature sets and training a Random Forest yields the best F1-score. In most cases, Random Forest performs better than SVM, which in turn works better on standalone EEG data.

5.2. Sentiment Classification

The third column of Table 2 describes the results for the sentiment classification task, where we have three possible classes. No model or feature combination provides a better performance than the text-based classifier in this setting. As in the sentiment detection task, Random Forest performs better in almost all cases. Only EEG data is again better processed using a linear SVM.

6. Discussion

Our experiments show that the biofeedback data we have collected contains information about the sentiment that the readers experience when reading the provided texts. Using only the readers' heart rates, we can achieve almost the same performance as a text-based classifier for the detection of sentiment in a text. Furthermore, we have shown that combining biofeedback features and lexicon-based text features can improve the overall performance over that of any of the components. Especially introducing EEG features yields a notable performance boost in comparison to heart rate plus text features. This suggests that, even though EEG features by themselves couldn't reach competitive performance levels, signals within this data help to enrich other feature sets.

We suggest that this finding can be used to facilitate the collection of annotations for long texts: In a first step, multiple users could be asked to read, for example, a full novel while collecting their biofeedback data. After that, a classifier based on the text and biofeedback can be used to detect emotional passages in the text, which can then be manually annotated for polarity or emotions. This would filter out sentences that do not contain emotions at all and therefore do not need to be labelled, saving a large amount of time for annotation. Since our biofeedback data was obtained using a consumer grade fitness watch and an affordable EEG headband, this approach scales well to a large number of annotators. It is important to note that higher quality electrodes, as well as semi-wet and wet EEG systems may lead to better results. However, despite higher-grade EEG systems may produce better data quality, we believe that enhancing the classification through our method is possible, and further, specifically applicable to consumer applications.

For the sentiment classification, our biofeedback based approach did not yield comparable results to the text based classification. The measured physiological arousal as well as the derived features and models did not capture *what* kind of emotion was felt but just *that* an emotion was felt. For the heart rate, this result is unsurprising, since a faster heart beat can come from a negative or positive excitement, such as being scared or falling in love. For EEG data, we would have expected different results, since EEG data has already been successfully incorporated in sentiment classification contexts (Kimmatkar and Babu, 2018). However, in contrast to our experimental setup, Kimmatkar and Babu (2018) used video-clips presented to a subject instead of text and recorded the EEG data using a 62 channel system instead of the 8 channel consumer grade OpenBCI system in our experiment. In addition, our EEG-based results only rely on one subject and one repetition whereas the aforementioned study had 15 participants repeat the experiments three times. Since Lakhan et al. (2019) suggest that in general consumer grade EEG systems such as OpenBCI can be used to detect emotions successfully, we hope to improve the performance by introducing more participants in the future, similar to the success of our human heart rate ensemble for sentiment detection.

As an additional point, we believe that biofeedback data presents a way of implicitly labelling sentences in relation to their context: medium-length texts, which are used in this study, consist of multiple sentences. While a sentence may seem neutral when judged in an isolated manner, the context of the text is very important to the person that is reading it. Biofeedback, such as heart rate or brain waves, does not just reflect the emotional state of the reader given the current sentence, but for the overall story up to that point. While many studies induced only one stimulus at a time (Choi et al., 2017; Lin et al., 2010; Gu et al., 2014), our study involved continuously reading sentences that build upon a given theme, for example humor or drama. Therefore, future labeling of sentences in texts should also consider the text before, such that the emotion that is currently induced by the text is better reflected.

This paper demonstrates a first approach, showing that biofeedback data can be used to improve text-based sentiment classifiers. Further studies will improve the data acquisition as well as processing. We are confident that the collection of a larger dataset and the inclusion of additional kinds of biofeedback will bring further improvements to the results in this first study.

7. Conclusion and Future Work

In this paper, we have presented an initial study about improving sentiment analysis tasks by incorporating biofeedback from subjects reading texts. We found that, while heart rate and EEG information was able to support machine learning models when detecting the presence of emotion in texts, it did not improve differentiation of said emotion as positive or negative.

In this work, we only measured physiological arousal using heart rate and EEG. In the future, we also plan to incorporate motor expression into the classification, which was, for example, proposed as classification input to analyze social interaction in virtual realities (Roth et al., 2019a). As reading usually does not induce sudden body movements, but possibly facial expressions reflecting the reader's emotions, additionally capturing and estimating them using the front camera of a smartphone is a promising option (Tarnowski et al., 2017), which will be implemented within the BioReader app. Introducing more complex text-based sentiment and emotion classifiers can also contribute to a better classification. Especially when facial expressions recorded by the front camera are introduced, multimodal systems such as MixedEmotions (Buitelaar et al., 2018) will be an interesting tool to study.

We also want to refine our evaluation scenario by collecting a larger dataset and labeling sentences such that the story context is captured. We believe that a larger scale EEG study can further reveal insights into the emotional thought process while reading texts. We plan to include more participants as well as complex features such as differential asymmetry (DASM) and rational asymmetry (RASM) (Duan et al., 2013) and we want to incorporate artificial neural networks using EEG data in the time domain, which are able to reflect features besides the frequency space.

8. Bibliographical References

Bhardwaj, A., Gupta, A., Jain, P., Rani, A., and Yadav, J. (2015). Classification of human emotions from eeg signals using svm and lda classifiers. In *2015 2nd International Conference on Signal Processing and Integrated Networks (SPIN)*, pages 180–185. IEEE.

Bos, D. O. et al. (2006). Eeg-based emotion recognition. *The Influence of Visual and Auditory Stimuli*, 56(3):1–17.

Buitelaar, P., Wood, I., Negi, S., Arčan, M., McCrae, J., Abele, A., Robin, C., Andryushechkin, V., Sagha, H., Schmitt, M., Schuller, B., Sánchez-Rada, J. F., Iglesias, C., Navarro, C., Giefer, A., Heise, N., Masucci, V., Danza, F., Caterino, C., and Ziad, H. (2018). Mixedemotions: An open-source toolbox for multi-modal emotion analysis. *IEEE Transactions on Multimedia*, PP:1–1, 01.

Caicedo, D. G. and Van Beuzekom, M. (2006). How do you feel? *An assessment of existing tools for the measurement of emotions and their application in consumer products research.*

Choi, K.-H., Kim, J., Kwon, O. S., Kim, M. J., Ryu, Y. H., and Park, J.-E. (2017). Is heart rate variability (hrv) an adequate tool for evaluating human emotions?–a focus on the use of the international affective picture system (iaps). *Psychiatry research*, 251:192–196.

Devlin, J., Chang, M.-W., Lee, K., and Toutanova, K. (2018). Bert: Pre-training of deep bidirectional transformers for language understanding. *arXiv preprint arXiv:1810.04805*.

Duan, R.-N., Zhu, J.-Y., and Lu, B.-L. (2013). Differential entropy feature for eeg-based emotion classification. In *2013 6th International IEEE/EMBS Conference on Neural Engineering (NER)*, pages 81–84. IEEE.

Gangula, R. R. R. and Mamidi, R. (2018). Resource creation towards automated sentiment analysis in telugu (a low resource language) and integrating multiple domain sources to enhance sentiment prediction. In *Proceedings of the Eleventh International Conference on Language Resources and Evaluation (LREC 2018)*.

Gu, Y., Celli, F., Steinberger, J., Anderson, A. J., Poesio, M., Strapparava, C., and Murphy, B. (2014). Using brain data for sentiment analysis. *JLCL*, 29:79–94.

Horlings, R., Datcu, D., and Rothkranz, L. J. M. (2008). Emotion recognition using brain activity. ACM.

Kimmatkar, N. V. and Babu, V. B. (2018). Human emotion classification from brain eeg signal using multimodal approach of classifier. In *Proceedings of the 2018 International Conference on Intelligent Information Technology*, pages 9–13.

Kobs, K., Zehe, A., Bernstetter, A., Chibane, J., Pfister, J., Tritscher, J., and Hotho, A. (2020). Emote-controlled: Obtaining implicit viewer feedback through emote based sentiment analysis on comments of popular twitch.tv channels. *ACM Transactions on Social Computing*.

Lakhan, P., Banluesombatkul, N., Changniam, V., Dhithijaiyratn, R., Leelaarporn, P., Boonchieng, E., Hompoonsup, S., and Wilaiprasitporn, T. (2019). Consumer grade brain sensing for emotion recognition. *IEEE Sensors Journal*, 19(21):9896–9907.

Lin, Y.-P., Wang, C.-H., Jung, T.-P., Wu, T.-L., Jeng, S.-K., Duann, J.-R., and Chen, J.-H. (2010). Eeg-based emotion recognition in music listening. *IEEE Transactions on Biomedical Engineering*, 57(7):1798–1806.

Munikar, M., Shakya, S., and Shrestha, A. (2019). Fine-grained sentiment classification using bert. In *2019 Artificial Intelligence for Transforming Business and Society (AITB)*, volume 1, pages 1–5. IEEE.

Murugappan, M. and Murugappan, S. (2013). Human emotion recognition through short time electroencephalogram (eeg) signals using fast fourier transform (fft). In *2013 IEEE 9th International Colloquium on Signal Processing and its Applications*, pages 289–294. IEEE.

Pedregosa, F., Varoquaux, G., Gramfort, A., Michel, V., Thirion, B., Grisel, O., Blondel, M., Prettenhofer, P., Weiss, R., Dubourg, V., Vanderplas, J., Passos, A., Cournapeau, D., Brucher, M., Perrot, M., and Duchesnay, E. (2011). Scikit-learn: Machine learning in Python. *Journal of Machine Learning Research*, 12:2825–2830.

Petrantonakis, P. C. and Hadjileontiadis, L. J. (2009). Emotion recognition from eeg using higher order crossings. *IEEE Transactions on information Technology in Biomedicine*, 14(2):186–197.

Picard, R. W. (2000). *Affective computing*. MIT press.

Rill, S., Reinel, D., Scheidt, J., and Zicari, R. V. (2014). Politwi: Early detection of emerging political topics on twitter and the impact on concept-level sentiment analysis. *Knowledge-Based Systems*, 69:24–33.

Roth, D., Bente, G., Kullmann, P., Mal, D., Purps, C. F., Vogeley, K., and Latoschik, M. E. (2019a). Technologies for social augmentations in user-embodied virtual reality. In *25th ACM Symposium on Virtual Reality Software and Technology*, pages 1–12.

Roth, D., Brübach, L., Westermeier, F., Schell, C., Feigl, T., and Latoschik, M. E. (2019b). A social interaction interface supporting affective augmentation based on neuronal data. In *Symposium on Spatial User Interaction*, pages 1–2.

Roth, D., Westermeier, F., Brübach, L., Feigl, T., Schell, C., and Latoschik, M. E. (2019c). Brain 2 communicate: Eeg-based affect recognition to augment virtual social interactions. In *Mensch und Computer 2019 - Workshopband*, Bonn. Gesellschaft für Informatik e.V.

Schlör, D., Veseli, B., and Hotho, A. (2019). Multimedia aus rezipientenperspektive: Wirkungsmessung anhand von biofeedback. *6. Tagung des Verbands Digital Humanities im deutschsprachigen Raum eV— DHd 2019: Digital Humanities multimedial & multimodal.*

Schmidt, T. and Burghardt, M. (2018). An evaluation of lexicon-based sentiment analysis techniques for the plays of gotthold ephraim lessing. In *Proceedings of the Second Joint SIGHUM Workshop on Computational Linguistics for Cultural Heritage, Social Sciences, Humanities and Literature*, pages 139–149.

Takahashi, K. (2004). Remarks on emotion recognition from bio-potential signals. In *2nd International conference on Autonomous Robots and Agents*, pages 186–191.

Tarnowski, P., Kolodziej, M., Majkowski, A., and Rak, R. J. (2017). Emotion recognition using facial expressions. In *ICCS*, pages 1175–1184.

Wang, H., Can, D., Kazemzadeh, A., Bar, F., and Narayanan, S. (2012). A system for real-time twitter sentiment analysis of 2012 us presidential election cycle. In *Proceedings of the ACL 2012 system demonstrations*, pages 115–120. Association for Computational Linguistics.

Zehe, A., Becker, M., Jannidis, F., and Hotho, A. (2017). Towards sentiment analysis on german literature. In *Joint German/Austrian Conference on Artificial Intelligence (Künstliche Intelligenz)*, pages 387–394. Springer.

Zhang, L., Wang, S., and Liu, B. (2018). Deep learning for sentiment analysis: A survey. *Wiley Interdisciplinary Reviews: Data Mining and Knowledge Discovery*, 8(4):e1253.

Association for Computational Linguistics
209 N. Eighth Street
Stroudsburg, Pennsylvania 18360

ISBN 978-1-7138-1271-5

CURRAN ASSOCIATES INC.
proceedings
.com